AMERICA the BEAUTIFUL

NORTH CAROLINA

By R. Conrad Stein

Consultants

Dale B. Thompson, Social Studies Demonstration Teacher, Alamance County Schools

Robert L. Hillerich, Ph.D., Bowling Green State University, Bowling Green, Ohio

CHILDRENS PRESS®
CHICAGO

Sea oats along the beach at Cape Hatteras

Project Editor: Joan Downing
Associate Editor: Shari Joffe
Design Director: Margrit Fiddle
Typesetting: Graphic Connections, Inc.
Engraving: Liberty Photoengraving

Library of Congress Cataloging-in-Publication Data

Stein, R. Conrad.
  America the beautiful. North Carolina / by R.
Conrad Stein.
     p.   cm.
  Includes index.
  Summary: Introduces the geography, history,
government, economy, industry, culture, historic
sites, and famous people of the Tar Heel State.
  ISBN 0-516-00479-4
  1. North Carolina—Juvenile literature.
[1. North Carolina.] I. Title.
F254.3.S74   1989   89-17298
975.6—dc20   CIP
                                           AC

**St. Peter's Church
and First Union
Center in Charlotte**

TABLE OF CONTENTS

Chapter   1   Welcome to the Tar Heel State 7

Chapter   2   The Land 9

Chapter   3   The People 19

Chapter   4   Foundations of a Colony 25

Chapter   5   The Second Century 41

Chapter   6   An Industrial Power 55

Chapter   7   Government and the Economy 69

Chapter   8   Arts and Recreation 79

Chapter   9   A Tar Heel Tour 91

Facts at a Glance 109

Maps 133

Index 138

Chapter 1

WELCOME TO
THE TAR HEEL STATE

WELCOME TO THE TAR HEEL STATE

An old story says that during the Revolutionary War, a red-coated army headed by British General Cornwallis marched through the colony of North Carolina. The colony's American patriots wanted to stop the British, so they dumped barrels of tar into a streambed that the British planned to cross. When Cornwallis's men and their horses splashed through the stream, their feet became covered with gooey tar, and they had to halt their march. A rumor may have then spread that anyone wading in North Carolina's streams would acquire "tar heels."

This Revolutionary War tale is one of many stories that attempt to explain how North Carolina got its nickname: the Tar Heel State. Whether the story is truth or myth, it illustrates the innovative nature of the Tar Heel people. North Carolinians are willing to embrace new ideas and are unafraid of taking chances. Their boldness has helped North Carolina become one of America's leading industrial states.

The Tar Heel State is also an uncommonly beautiful place to visit. So diverse are its landforms that in the winter, vacationers may ski over snow-covered slopes at one end of the state, while in the summer, they can enjoy the seashore at the opposite end. It is no wonder that the state tourist office calls North Carolina the Variety Vacationland.

North Carolina welcomes the student, too. Its rich culture and history make it one of the most interesting members of the American family. North Carolinians' confidence in their state and its institutions is reflected in the official state motto: *Esse Quam Videri*, "To Be Rather Than To Seem."

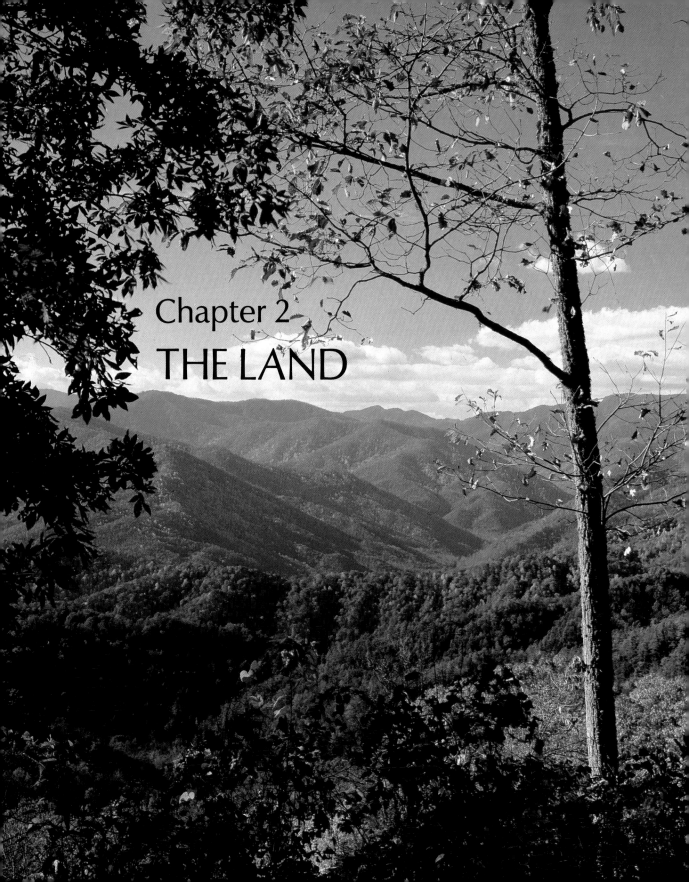

Chapter 2
THE LAND

THE LAND

*It [North Carolina] is almost wholly forest,
with indescribably beautiful cedar wood,
poplars, oaks, beech, walnut . . . and so many
other fragrant trees that I cannot describe
the hundredth part.*
—Christen Janzen, a New Bern settler writing in 1711

GEOGRAPHY

North Carolina is a South Atlantic state. It is bounded by Virginia to the north, Tennessee to the west, South Carolina and Georgia to the south, and the Atlantic Ocean to the east and southeast. Long and narrow in shape, the state's greatest east-west distance is 503 miles (809 kilometers). From north to south, its longest distance is 187 miles (301 kilometers). North Carolina's area is 52,669 square miles (136,413 square kilometers), making it twenty-eighth in size among the states.

Raleigh is the Tar Heel State's capital; Charlotte is its largest city.

THE THREE NORTH CAROLINAS

North Carolina has three distinct and dramatically different land regions: the Atlantic Coastal Plain, the Piedmont Plateau, and the Mountain Region. These regions shaped the state's past and affect its current development.

The Atlantic Coastal Plain is a long belt of land that extends from New Jersey to Florida along the ocean shore. Nearly half of North Carolina's land lies in the Atlantic Coastal Plain. The land here is flat; the soil is moist. The region is home to the state's richest farmland as well as to swamps and marshes. The great Dismal Swamp, a wildly beautiful wetland despite its name, lies in the northern coastal plain and spills into Virginia.

To the west of the coastal plain, stretching from Delaware to Alabama, is the Piedmont Plateau. In North Carolina, the Piedmont is about 200 miles (322 kilometers) wide. Ranging in altitude from 500 to 1,500 feet (152 to 457 meters), the Piedmont is the "doorstep" of the Appalachian Mountains. The land is hilly and the soil is predominantly red clay. The cities along the Piedmont Plateau are centers for the state's commerce and industry. More North Carolinians live in the Piedmont than in the other two regions combined.

The Mountain Region, west of the Piedmont, is dominated by two ranges: the Blue Ridge Mountains and the Great Smoky Mountains. Both ranges are part of the Appalachian chain, which runs like a jagged fence from the Canadian province of Quebec to Alabama. The Blue Ridge peaks today look much as they did 200 million years ago. These old mountains are round-shouldered and cloaked with forests even at the highest elevations. Mount Mitchell, at 6,684 feet (2,037 meters), is the highest point in North Carolina and the tallest peak east of the Mississippi River. Great Smoky Mountains National Park, which extends into Tennessee, is a scenic highlight of the beautiful Mountain Region.

THE SEACOAST

North Carolina has about 301 miles (484 kilometers) of seacoast. Much of the coast is made up of gentle beaches that

Cape Hatteras, part of the area known as the Outer Banks, has the tallest lighthouse in the United States.

invite swimming. But the often peaceful waters may mask submerged shoals and treacherous currents.

The long, narrow islands that lie off the shoreline are called the Outer Banks. Four centuries ago, English-speaking civilization in the New World began at North Carolina's Roanoke Island. Sometime later, pirates used several of the islands as lairs. Between the Outer Banks and the shore stretch calm, shallow bands of water called *sounds*. Numerous small islands rest in the sounds.

North Carolina's seacoast includes many capes. A cape is a long, slender, often sandy peninsula that extends into the sea. Three prominent capes—Hatteras, Lookout, and Fear—jut into North Carolina's coastal waters. For centuries, ships have used the calm waters created by the capes as "highways" through which to sail into the state's major ports—Morehead City, Beaufort, and Wilmington. But as the names *Lookout* and *Fear* imply, the capes' shifting sands can cause shipwrecks. Indeed, Cape Hatteras is known as the "Graveyard of the Atlantic."

RIVERS AND LAKES

Most of North Carolina's major rivers have sources in the
Mountain Region or in the Piedmont. The rivers flow south or
southeast and eventually empty into the Atlantic Ocean. Large
southward-flowing rivers include the Cape Fear, Neuse, Pamlico,
Roanoke, and Chowan rivers. These waterways change character
as they run through the state's three major land regions. The
rivers of the mountains are swift, and the region enjoys many
beautiful waterfalls. As the rivers cross the rocky land of the
Piedmont Plateau, they tend to be fast-flowing and have narrow
channels. After the rivers pass the Fall Line—the sharp downward
slope that separates the Piedmont Plateau from the Atlantic
Coastal Plain—they become broader and lazier.

North Carolina's largest lakes were created artificially by dams
in the river system. Lake Norman, Lake Hickory, and High Rock
Lake are major man-made lakes that lie wholly within the state.
Boggs Lake, part of the Kerr Reservoir system, is shared with

Above: Gulls along the North Carolina coast
Right: Wildflowers in the Piedmont

Virginia. All of the state's large natural lakes are found on the
Atlantic Coastal Plain. Lake Mattamuskeet, near the Pamlico
River, is the state's largest natural lake.

PLANTS AND ANIMALS

Almost two-thirds of North Carolina is forest covered.
Lumbering and the manufacture of wood products have long been
among the state's major industries. Common trees include cedars,
pines, maples, oaks, tulip trees, tupelos, and hickories. North
Carolina's geographic diversity allows for both subarctic trees,
such as the spruces and balsams of the high mountains; and
subtropical species, such as the palmettos of the southern coastal
areas. In the moist, coastal region stand graceful cypresses. Often
growing in shallow lakes with their root systems exposed, the
cypresses look as if they are standing on their tiptoes.

Both beautiful wildflowers (left) and an occasional black bear (above) can be spotted in the Mountain Region.

In the spring, North Carolina is ablaze with wildflowers. Azaleas and rhododendrons blanket city gardens and grow freely in the wild. Camellias, redbuds, and dogwoods herald early spring, while the beardtongue—so named because of its whiskery tip—blooms in June and July. The mountain laurel, which explodes into brilliant white and pink flowers, grows to a height of 15 feet (4.6 meters) in the western mountains. Orchids bloom along the coastal plain. Also on the coastal plain grows the exotic Venus's-flytrap. Found only in the South Atlantic region of the country, the Venus's-flytrap lures flies and other insects onto its leaves, then closes them like a trap and devours its prey.

Deer roam the woods throughout the state. Black bears are found mainly in the Mountain Region. Beavers build sturdy dams in the state's streams. Other small animals include otters, foxes, rabbits, opossums, raccoons, and skunks. In freshwater rivers and lakes swim bass, bluegills, trout, and sunfish. Off the Atlantic

The beginnings of a storm along the coast near Rodanthe

coast are marlin, sailfish, menhaden, and dolphins. The cardinal is North Carolina's state bird. Huge flocks of ducks and geese winter in the marshlands of the coastal plain and the Outer Banks. Mockingbirds, Carolina wrens, mourning doves, woodcocks, and partridges nest throughout the state.

An interesting animal unique to the Outer Banks is the small but hardy wild pony. Thought to be descendants of Spanish mustangs, the ponies have splashed through the salt marshes and raced over sand dunes for nearly four centuries. Though they once numbered about 2,000, now only about 150 horses roam Ocracoke Island and the Cape Lookout National Seashore. Unfortunately, as more houses are built in the Outer Banks, the animals' rangeland is diminished and their numbers decline.

CLIMATE

North Carolina's climate varies among the three major land regions. The Atlantic Coastal Plain has the warmest winter temperatures as well as hot, often uncomfortable, summers. Though cooler weather prevails year-round in the western mountains, the winters there are still short and mild. Some parts of the Mountain Region may experience short-lived but significant snowfall. In contrast, snowfall is rare along the coast. The climate of the Piedmont Plateau ranges between that of the mountains and the coastal plain. Winter days on the Piedmont Plateau are often brisk, but rarely freezing. Charlotte, in the heart of the Piedmont Plateau, has an average January temperature of 43 degrees Fahrenheit (6 degrees Celsius); in July, the city's average temperature is 79 degrees Fahrenheit (26 degrees Celsius).

North Carolina farmers usually enjoy ample rainfall. Rain is heaviest along the coast and in the western mountains. The disastrous nationwide drought of 1988 withered many crops on the Piedmont Plateau, but most farmers on the coastal plain experienced sufficient rain.

On occasion, nature unleashes violent weather on North Carolina. Deadly twisters raked the Piedmont Plateau in 1984 and 1988. The 1988 tornado killed five people in the Raleigh area. Hurricanes often lash the North Carolina coast. A 1954 hurricane that killed nineteen people was such an awesome event that the residents have dated their lives around it. Along the coast, people still say, "I was in the seventh grade when the hurricane hit," or "We'd been married a month when the hurricane destroyed our house."

Despite nature's occasional outbursts, the Tar Heel State has generally cheery weather and land that is a delight to behold. A typical day in the state begins bright and sunny, making a song that was written in the 1920s still ring true today:

Nothin' can be finer
Than to be in Carolina in the morning.

Chapter 3
THE PEOPLE

THE PEOPLE

These [North Carolinians] are hard-working people who
look before they leap.... It's a state of individuals.
—Sam Ervin, a longtime North Carolina senator

POPULATION AND POPULATION DISTRIBUTION

In terms of population, North Carolina ranks tenth among the
fifty states; the 1980 census listed North Carolina's population at
5,881,813. This figure represents an increase of 16 percent over the
1970 census figure. By 1985, the state's population was estimated
at 6,225,000. Much of this population growth is due to migration,
as thriving industries and a bright employment picture draw
people to North Carolina.

North Carolina is one of the few states in which rural dwellers
are in the majority. About 52 percent of the people in North
Carolina live in rural areas—on farms and in small towns and
communities. In contrast, rural dwellers make up only 25 percent
of America's population as a whole. Nevertheless, the population
distribution of North Carolina is slowly changing. As more North
Carolinians move to the cities in search of work, the rural
population is decreasing. This, along with the continued
migration of people into the state, will soon push the urban-
dwelling population beyond the current 48 percent.

The greatest concentration of people occurs in the cities of the
industrialized Piedmont Plateau. Raleigh, Durham, Greensboro,
and Winston-Salem stretch along the north-central part of the
Piedmont, each city lying about an hour's drive from the next.

Charlotte, which lies in the southern part of the Piedmont, is the state's largest city, with a population of 314,447. About 1.4 million people live within a 56-mile (90-kilometer) radius of Charlotte's center. North Carolina's other major cities are, in order of population, Greensboro, Raleigh, Winston-Salem, Durham, High Point, Fayetteville, and Asheville.

WHO ARE THE NORTH CAROLINIANS?

For generations, North Carolina has experienced little immigration by people from foreign countries. Today, 99 percent of the state's people were born in the United States. Most residents are descendants of the state's original English, Scotch-Irish, German, and black settlers. About 1 percent of the state's people are of Hispanic origin, and slightly less than 1 percent are of Asian descent. The few North Carolinians who were not born in the United States come from such countries as Canada, Germany, Great Britain, Korea, and Japan.

About 22 percent of North Carolinians are black. Before World War II, blacks made up nearly 30 percent of the population. During and after the war, however, many blacks abandoned North Carolina because they suffered unemployment and discrimination. In recent years, blacks have begun to return to the Tar Heel State, drawn by the state's industrial expansion. Furthermore, many of the laws and customs that once restricted blacks' rights have long been rescinded.

More than sixty thousand Native Americans (American Indians) live in North Carolina, making up about 1 percent of the state's population. Native Americans reside throughout the state, but many live on the Cherokee Indian Reservation in the mountainous western tip of the state. The Qualla Cherokee Indian

Boundary, as it is officially known, is North Carolina's only Indian reservation. Its residents make up the Eastern Band of the Cherokee Nation.

REGIONALISM

An elderly woman from North Carolina's Blue Ridge Mountains crossed the length of the state to see the Atlantic Ocean for the first time in her life. After the visit she said, "There's water and earth, and during Creation the Lord divided them one from the other. I'm of the notion that we're divided up that way too: into water folks and hill folks. I'm at home in the hills . . . but I'm a true stranger to water and water's ways."

Regionalism, as summed up by the woman's statement, is an everyday fact of life in North Carolina. Some residents would live nowhere else but along the coast, while others feel comfortable only when surrounded by their familiar mountains. Longtime residents can easily detect the accents and speech patterns that have developed over the years in the different regions. These regional traits, which have evolved over the past few hundred years, extend to such matters as voting patterns and food preferences.

The culture of the coastal plain is linked closely to that of the Old South. The few plantations that developed in North Carolina before the Civil War were located in the coastal area. Today, the coast remains a place where life proceeds at a leisurely pace and where people pride themselves on their dignity and courtly manners. People living in the Piedmont are, in comparison, sometimes perceived as being in a hurry. This is perhaps because the Piedmont is the most "citified" of the state's three regions. For many years, people of the Blue Ridge Mountains lived in splendid isolation because few roads linked them with their flatland neighbors. Over the years, the mountaineers developed a regional dialect that included such double-noun expressions as "tooth dentist" and "widow woman."

Regionalism depends, in part, on the continued separation of the people of different regions. But modern North Carolina has excellent roads, and its people travel far more frequently than did their ancestors. As a result, regional attitudes and traits are quickly breaking down. Many observers of the state point out sadly that as North Carolinians lose their regional identities, a little bit of the state's color and charm is lost as well.

RELIGION

Baptists make up the state's largest religious group. Other major Christian denominations followed in North Carolina include Methodism, Presbyterianism, and Roman Catholicism.

Religion is a passion among many North Carolinians. The state is a center of Fundamentalist belief. Fundamentalists claim that every sentence in the Bible must be taken as literal truth. A large number of North Carolinians are Evangelicals who find great joy in spreading the word of the Bible.

Perhaps the world's most famous evangelist is Billy Graham, who was born in Charlotte and remains a North Carolina resident. *Time* magazine has called Graham "America's most admired religious leader." During his long career, Graham has preached in person to more than 100 million people.

Some people hold that one American state is much like another. North Carolinians disagree. Uniqueness is the mark of the Tar Heel State—and the state can trace its uniqueness to its proud past.

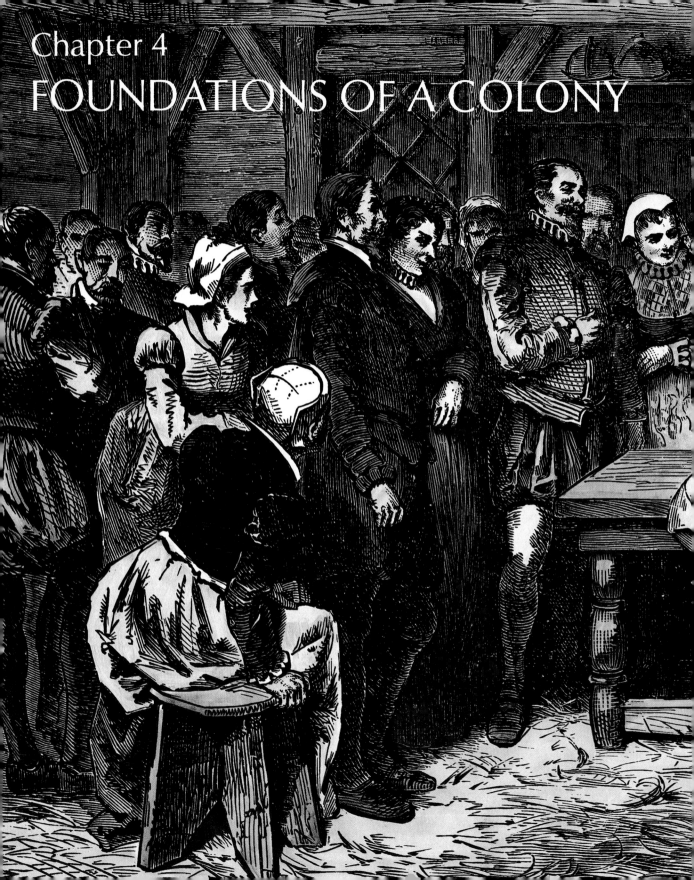

FOUNDATIONS OF A COLONY

THE FIRST NORTH CAROLINIANS

About ten thousand years ago, bands of hunters entered what is now North Carolina. The hunters were descendants of a great wave of people who had migrated from Asia to North America when the Ice Age still gripped the earth. These ancient people hunted deer, buffalo, and perhaps even mammoths. They moved from place to place, following the animal herds and using spears to bring down their prey. At Morrow Mountain, near the present-day town of Albemarle, are stone outcrops from which ancient hunters chipped off spear points.

Gradually, as the climate of the region changed, the peoples' habits changed as well. They began to catch fish and to trap smaller animals for food.

Archaeologists believe that about two thousand years ago, people living in North Carolina had begun to farm. Farming allowed these woodland people to establish villages. They could now keep fires burning long enough to make clay cooking pots and other ceramic items. Evidence suggests that the Indians of the South Atlantic area were the first North Americans east of the Mississippi River to use pottery.

THE CONTACT PERIOD

In the 1500s, when Europeans first arrived in North America, about thirty tribes or culture groups lived in the North Carolina

When English colonist John White came to North Carolina in 1585, he made many drawings of the Native Americans he encountered, including these sketches of an Indian village (above) and the way the Indians fished (left).

region. Each group might have several villages scattered throughout an area. The first group encountered by the Europeans were the Croatans. The Croatans, also known as the Hatteras, lived along the Outer Banks. The Tuscaroras, the most powerful group in the North Carolina region, lived on the coastal plain and in the Piedmont. The Pamlico and the Coree also lived on the coastal plain. The Piedmont was the home of the Cheraw, the Keyauwee, the Catawba, and the Waxhaw. The Cherokee lived in the Blue Ridge Mountains. More than thirty-five thousand people were living in what is now North Carolina when the first European explorers arrived.

Customs varied from region to region, but the Native Americans of North Carolina shared some common traits. Most of them lived in small villages near a river or the seacoast. Their houses were made of sapling frames covered with bark or animal skins. They hunted and fished, and they grew corn, white potatoes, squash, and beans. The people believed in good and evil spirits. Festivals to celebrate the harvest or the planting season featured dancing and sometimes a long fast followed by a feast. Medicine men or village elders treated patients with prayers and chants and by administering tonics made from roots and herbs.

Although there was no formal written language, the people were excellent map readers. Shells were used as a form of money; different colors of shells had different values. The coastal tribes called the shell money *ronoak*.

THE NEW LAND

" . . . there appeared [before us] a new land which had never been seen by any man, either ancient or modern," reads the logbook of sea captain Giovanni da Verrazano, who sailed past Cape Fear in 1524 while exploring the area for France. Verrazano and his crew are believed to have been the first Europeans to gaze upon North Carolina's shores. Other Europeans followed Verrazano and explored the South Atlantic coast.

Spanish explorer Hernando De Soto, leading an army of six hundred soldiers, reached North Carolina by land from Florida in 1540. The main purpose of De Soto's expedition was to find the fantastic stores of gold he thought existed in the New World. It is believed that De Soto entered the Blue Ridge Mountains and made contact with the Cherokee people before continuing westward.

British nobleman Sir Walter Raleigh is often called the "father

This 1590 engraving, made after a lost drawing by John White, shows the first group of English settlers arriving at Roanoke Island in 1585.

of English-speaking America," even though he never journeyed to what is now the United States. Instead, Raleigh sponsored exploration and colonization missions to the new land. The first exploring party sent by Raleigh was headed by sea captains Philip Amadas and Arthur Barlowe. In 1584, the two captains landed at the North Carolina island "the Indians call Roanoke." Overwhelmed by the lush forests, the men returned to England and reported, "[There] the earth bringeth forth all things in abundance, as in the first creation, without toil or labor."

After hearing the glowing reports, Raleigh sent another expedition to the region. Several ships and several hundred men, led by Ralph Lane, reached Hatteras in the Outer Banks in late 1585. These settlers established a colony at Roanoke Island.

The colony was plagued with problems from the very start. Many of the colonists were more interested in searching for gold than in building houses and planting crops. Worse yet, Lane and his men antagonized the local Indians, and a full-scale war loomed. After less than a year on Roanoke Island, Lane and the discouraged colonists returned to England.

THE LOST COLONY

Undaunted, Sir Walter Raleigh sent a second group of settlers to Roanoke Island in 1587. This expedition, led by John White, included fourteen families. In August of 1587, Eleanor Dare, the daughter of John White, gave birth to a baby girl. Christened Virginia Dare, the baby was the first child born of English parents on American soil.

The colonists had arrived too late in the year to plant and harvest crops before the coming winter. Shortly after Virginia's birth, John White sailed to England to obtain additional supplies for the colony. Though White reached England safely, a war between Spain and England prevented him from returning to the colony for three years. When he finally set foot on Roanoke Island, John White was shocked to discover that the houses and grounds of the outpost were deserted. The only clue left behind was the word *Croatoan* carved into a tree. White planned to search for the colonists, but a fierce storm arose, badly damaging his ship. He was forced to return to England, puzzling over the fate of his friends and family. No member of the colony was ever heard from again.

What happened to the people of the Lost Colony remains a mystery. Many historians believe that the English colonists were killed by hostile Indians or by marauding Spaniards. Others theorize that the colonists simply joined the Croatan people. These historians point out that many Lumbee Indians, who are descendants of the Croatan and still live in southeastern North Carolina, have the same last names as the colonists who disappeared.

THE FIRST SETTLERS

North Carolina is sometimes called the "State Without a Birthday" because it is not known exactly when the first Europeans settled there permanently. The earliest Europeans to establish farms in North Carolina came in the mid-1600s from the English colony of Virginia, which had been founded in 1607. The forested land to the south and west of Virginia had been known as *Carolana* (Latin for "Land of Charles") since 1629, when King Charles I of England granted the region to his attorney general, Sir Robert Heath. Carolana (the spelling was later changed to *Carolina*) was a huge strip of land that included both present-day North Carolina and South Carolina and stretched all the way to the Pacific Ocean. Heath did little to develop this vast region.

North Carolina's oldest-recorded land transaction occurred in 1660, when Virginian Nathaniel Batts purchased land near the Chowan River from King Kisqutanewh of the Weapemeoc tribe. One year later, George Durant made a similar purchase. The present-day community of Durant's Neck is a reminder of that long-ago exchange.

By the late 1600s, more than five hundred settlers and their families worked small farms in what is now North Carolina. Most of the settlers staked out their holdings along Albemarle Sound, where the Chowan River empties into the Atlantic. Today this region is called the "Cradle of North Carolina."

In 1663, Charles II of England revoked Heath's title to Carolina and granted the region to eight English noblemen. They became the *lords proprietors* (ruling landowners) of the colony. The lords proprietors, who remained in England, appointed a governor to rule the colony.

The settlers resented being ruled by the absent lords proprietors, who showed little concern for the colonists. In 1677, led by a land surveyor and local official named John Culpeper, the colonists overthrew the English governor. For about a year after "Culpeper's Rebellion," the colonists governed themselves.

North Carolina's early growth was slow. The region lacked an adequate seaport, and travel over land from Virginia meant crossing swampland or broad rivers. By 1710, about three thousand European settlers were living in the region. It had only three towns—Bath, Edenton, and New Bern. Bath, established in 1705, was the region's first town. Edenton served as the seat of government. New Bern was founded in 1710 by a party of 650 German and Swiss immigrants seeking religious freedom.

As the colony developed, the Indians retreated as whites encroached upon the lands that the Indians had used for centuries. Considering the relentlessness of the white onslaught, surprisingly few conflicts broke out in those initial days of settlement. John Lawson, a famous writer of early North Carolina history, said of the Indians, "They are really better to us than we are to them."

The Tuscarora Indians were among the most well-organized in the North Carolina region. They traded with the other Indian groups, and when the Europeans arrived, they established a profitable trade with them as well. However, the lords proprietors eventually passed laws that prohibited the Tuscarora from trading with anyone but the English. This, along with the founding of

In the early 1700s, pirates such as Anne Bonney and Mary Read used the Outer Banks as a hideout from which to spring upon commercial ships.

New Bern on what had been Tuscarora territory, angered the Indians. They began to fear that they would lose all their land to the Europeans. In 1711, the bloody Tuscarora War broke out. For two years, the Tuscarora warriors and the colonists fought. Villages were burned and hundreds of settlers and Indians were killed before the Tuscarora were defeated.

Violence also reigned off the Outer Banks, which had become a hotbed of piracy. Small, fast pirate ships commanded by ruthless captains used North Carolina's chain of islands to hide in and then spring upon commercial ships. Two infamous pirates who scourged the North Carolina coast were women—Anne Bonney and Mary Read. The most feared of all the pirates, however, was Edward Teach, better known as Blackbeard. Based in the town of Bath, Blackbeard matched the Hollywood image of a bloodthirsty buccaneer. His thick, braided beard made his face look particularly devilish, and he was never seen without three pistols stuck in his belt. In 1718, Blackbeard was killed in a battle on North Carolina's Ocracoke Island.

THE COLONY COMES OF AGE

For almost a hundred years, the lands that eventually became North Carolina and South Carolina were considered by the English government to be one colony. In 1712, the colony was divided into North Carolina and South Carolina, and each was appointed its own governor. In 1729, King George III of England purchased the land grants from the lords proprietors, and North Carolina officially became a royal colony. At about the same time, North Carolina resolved a complicated boundary dispute with Virginia.

The new colony of North Carolina was settled not by immigrants coming directly from Europe, but by the overflow from its colonial neighbors. The vast majority of newcomers were from Virginia, South Carolina, or Pennsylvania. As more and more settlers arrived, the towns of Beaufort and Brunswick developed. With the founding of Wilmington in 1730, North Carolina finally gained a port city.

Among the boldest of the North Carolina pioneers were the Scotch-Irish, who left the Scottish hill country to settle first in Ireland and then in the New World. Hundreds of Scotch-Irish came to North Carolina from Pennsylvania over wilderness trails. The colony's most celebrated Scotch-Irish pioneer was Daniel Boone. Boone's parents built a log cabin in North Carolina's Blue Ridge Mountains in 1751, when Boone was still a youth. From this base, Boone explored the untamed Kentucky territory, and eventually founded the outpost of Boonesboro.

The town of Salem, depicted here in a 1787 painting by Ludwig Gottfried von Redeken, was founded in 1766 by Moravians seeking religious freedom.

North Carolina's settler population increased from about 30,000 in 1730 to about 350,000 in 1775. Although most of the people lived on the coastal plain, many towns developed in the Piedmont. Fayetteville, originally called Campbelltown, was founded by Scottish Highlanders about 1730. Charlotte was founded in the 1760s, when English and Scotch-Irish farmers named their newly built village for Queen Charlotte, wife of King George III. The town of Salem was founded in 1766 by Moravians seeking religious freedom. Nearly a century passed before the neighboring city of Winston was born, and still later, the two towns merged.

North Carolina, largely a land of small farms, offered a sharp contrast to the huge cotton and tobacco plantations that sprawled across neighboring South Carolina and Virginia. Tobacco use had been growing in popularity in Europe ever since Christopher Columbus observed Caribbean natives smoking the leaves through clay pipes they called *tobagos*. Many North Carolina

These early engravings illustrate how tar was made in North Carolina by scraping pine trees to collect rosin (left) and then heating the rosin in a kiln (right).

farmers recognized the opportunity and grew tobacco as a cash crop. Nearly all North Carolina farmers planted grain and raised cattle and hogs.

The colony's first major industry was the production of tar, pitch, and turpentine. These items, used in building and maintaining ships, were collectively called *naval stores*. Tar and turpentine were products of North Carolina's endless pine forests. The early production of tar is one explanation for how the state received its nickname.

Some settlers who came to North Carolina brought slaves. Slavery and the slave trade had occurred throughout the English colonies since 1619. In North Carolina, slaves were valuable to the plantations that developed on the coastal plain. However, the small farmers of the Piedmont and the pioneers who pushed into the Blue Ridge Mountains did not rely on slave labor. As a result, slavery never became as deeply entrenched an institution in North Carolina as it did in South Carolina and Virginia.

Politically, the colony was dominated by the wealthy plantation owners of the coastal region. Although there were only about a dozen of them, these aristocrats controlled local government, influenced the collection of taxes, and commanded the colonial militia. Small farmers in the Piedmont resisted this domination by forming a group called the Regulators, whose members vowed to "regulate public grievances and abuses of power." At the Battle of Alamance Creek, fought in 1771 near Hillsborough, the Regulators suffered a heroic defeat at the hands of the colonial militia.

By the late 1770s, the government of England emerged as North Carolina's foremost foe. The British treasury had been drained by the Seven Years' War (known in North America as the French and Indian War), which had ended in 1763. To raise money, England levied heavier taxes on its American colonies. The Stamp Act, which placed a tax on legal documents, was particularly hated in North Carolina. To protest the taxes, many North Carolinians joined a secret society. Known as the Sons of Liberty, it advocated rebellion against the mother country. In open defiance of British rule, bands of North Carolina colonists met in New Bern to elect delegates to the First Continental Congress, which was forming in Philadelphia. The Revolutionary War broke out in 1775, and in April 1776, North Carolina became the first colony to instruct its Continental Congress delegates to vote for independence.

WAR, PEACE, AND STATEHOOD

Movies often portray the American Revolution as a great patriotic effort that pitted all Americans against their British overlords. The truth is that the colonists were a sharply divided people during their war of independence. Many colonists—

including thousands of North Carolinians—preferred to stay loyal to the British Crown rather than rebel against the mother country.

As was true in the other colonies, North Carolinians who remained loyal to Britain were called *loyalists*, or *Tories*, while those advocating independence became known as *patriots*, or *Whigs*. The first battle fought on North Carolina soil was waged not by colonists against Great Britain, but by North Carolina Tories against North Carolina Whigs. The battle, which took place at Moores Creek Bridge near Wilmington in February 1776, resulted in an overwhelming Whig victory. Commanding the Whig forces was Colonel Richard Caswell, who later became the state's first governor. The Tory defeat prevented the British from landing troops at Wilmington and capturing the colony.

North Carolina provided about six thousand soldiers for the Continental (American) army. In addition, some ten thousand North Carolinians enrolled as militiamen. Few battles were fought on North Carolina soil. One North Carolina battle, however, was a turning point in the war. On March 15, 1781, at Guilford Courthouse, the troops of American General Nathanael Greene clashed with British forces led by Lord Charles Cornwallis. Though the British won the battle, they came away severely weakened. Later, Cornwallis attempted to evacuate his troops from the South. Unable to accomplish this, he was forced to surrender at Yorktown, Virginia, in October 1781.

Although North Carolinians had been eager to vote for independence, they were more cautious when it came to adopting the United States Constitution. Many of the voters—small farmers who feared a powerful central government—initially refused to ratify the document. At the Hillsborough Convention of 1788, North Carolina delegates suggested a number of changes in the Constitution, some of which were incorporated into the

In the 1820s, Raleigh artist Jacob Marling painted this view of North Carolina's first state house.

document's Bill of Rights. In 1789, North Carolina delegates met at Fayetteville, and this time voted to accept the United States Constitution. The act of ratification officially made North Carolina the twelfth state to enter the Union.

North Carolina's state constitution, written during the war years, tended to favor the wealthy planters. Some voting privileges were restricted to landowners. Though the colony had freed itself of British rule, many North Carolinians still had little or no voice in their government.

The state's first official capital was New Bern, but during the war years, the legislature met at New Bern, Hillsborough, Smithfield, Halifax, Fayetteville, and Tarboro. Finally, in 1792, the state bought 1,000 acres (405 hectares) of land near the Wake County Courthouse, and the capital city of Raleigh was born.

Chapter 5
THE SECOND CENTURY

THE SECOND CENTURY

After the Revolutionary War, North Carolina's leaders addressed the need for higher education in the state. Led by William R. Davie, called the "father of the university," the state legislature chartered the University of North Carolina at what is now Chapel Hill. Opened in 1795, the school was America's first state university. It seemed as if North Carolina was well on its way to becoming a dynamic and aggressive state.

But progress came slowly to North Carolina. In fact, early in the 1800s, the state gained the nickname "Rip Van Winkle State." By some accounts, North Carolina seemed to be asleep while its nearest neighbors gained wealth and prestige. Virginia and South Carolina were the leading powers in the South, and it was often said that North Carolina was a "valley of humility between two mountains of conceit."

Poor transportation was a major cause of the state's slow development. North Carolina is an unusually long state from east to west, but most of its rivers—the chief highways of commerce in the early 1800s—flowed across its narrow north-south width. Shipping goods from the eastern coastal plain to the western mountains was an expensive undertaking. As a result, North Carolina's economy was at a standstill. Furthermore, politics in the state were dominated by one small group—the eastern planters. As long as their own interests were served, these leaders saw little reason to change or improve the conditions in the western part of the state.

Meanwhile, more and more people were moving westward to settle in the Blue Ridge and on the Piedmont Plateau. By 1800, Rowan County, in the Piedmont, had a population twice that of any eastern county. Yet the wealthy planters in the east continued to dominate state politics.

As the state languished, thousands of residents looked for opportunities elsewhere. In 1829, an Asheville newspaperman reported seeing eight to fifteen westbound wagons a day. North Carolina's population dropped from third in the nation in 1790 to seventh by 1840. Among those who left the state were three future presidents: Andrew Jackson, James Polk, and Andrew Johnson.

TRAIL OF TEARS

The westward movement of the white settlers through North Carolina eventually brought them to Cherokee lands. In the past, contact with white settlers had meant trouble for the Cherokee. In the 1730s, nearly half of the Cherokee population had died from smallpox brought by the Europeans. In 1759, the colonists and the Cherokee had fought over lands occupied by the Cherokee. The war ended and the Cherokee signed a treaty allowing colonists to move into the easternmost parts of the mountain region. But the colonists soon spread beyond the treaty's boundaries. Another treaty, drawn up in 1785, was also broken by the white settlers. As time went on, the Cherokee were forced to give up more and more land.

Settlers throughout the eastern part of the country were moving westward. In the 1830s, the federal government decided to relocate the Cherokee, as well as other eastern tribes, to lands west of the Mississippi River. The federal army forced the Cherokee to walk more than 1,000 miles (1,609 kilometers) from North

Plank roads, which became known as "farmers' railroads," were built across the length of North Carolina in the mid-1800s.

Carolina to present-day Oklahoma. The forced march was bitter and cruel; along the way, nearly one-fourth of the Indians died of starvation, sickness, and exposure to the cold. The survivors of this march called it the "Trail of Tears."

About a thousand Cherokee hid in the North Carolina mountains and fought to stay on their land. The leader of this band, Tsali, was captured and executed. His followers, however, were allowed to remain in North Carolina. Today, those lands are known as the Qualla Cherokee Indian Boundary.

LEAPING AHEAD

In 1835, a convention met in Raleigh to revise the state constitution. Over the objections of the eastern landowners, new provisions gave political strength to the people of the western part

of the state. The revised constitution stimulated business and cultural activities.

The small farmers of the Piedmont used their newly gained power to demand better transportation across the state. In response, the state government chartered companies to build a network of plank roads across the length of the state. Because these plank roads allowed small farmers to bring goods to market, they became known as "farmers' railroads." The new government also encouraged railroad construction. The state's first railroad line, completed in 1840, linked Wilmington with Weldon. Stretching 161 miles (259 kilometers), it was said to be the longest continuous railroad track in the world at that time.

North Carolina's first public schools opened in 1840, and within ten years, a hundred thousand students attended regular classes. Heading the school system was a dedicated educator, Calvin H.

Until 1829, all of the native gold coined by the United States Mint was mined in North Carolina (right). Christopher Bechtler, who opened a private mint in Rutherfordton in 1831, stamped the nation's first gold dollars (above).

Wiley. According to historian H. G. Jones, Wiley gave North Carolina the "best state system of public education in the South." Private colleges such as Wake Forest, Davidson, and Trinity (now Duke University) opened during the same period.

The provisions of the 1835 constitution woke the state from its economic slumber. By 1850, the state was on its way to becoming one of the most prosperous in the South. Between 1850 and 1860, the production of agricultural products increased dramatically. Cotton and wheat production doubled, and tobacco production tripled. The value of manufactured goods increased by more than 70 percent. By 1860, the state had 900 miles (1,448 kilometers) of railroad track.

Gold mining was the state's most exciting industry. Gold had been discovered decades earlier in the Piedmont when a boy named Conrad Reed chanced upon a large glittering rock. Because he did not know its value, Reed's father at first used the rock as a doorstop for his cabin. However, others soon discovered the gold deposit, and prospectors poured into the Piedmont region.

THE SLAVERY QUESTION

"Land And Negroes For Sale," read a sign posted near the Stokes County Courthouse in 1836. The sign also announced the sale of "corn, oats, and horses," along with "seven Negroes, consisting of men, women, and children."

In years before the Civil War, about 30 percent of North Carolina's population was black. The overwhelming majority of those blacks were slaves. Despite these numbers, slavery was not as firmly entrenched in North Carolina as it was in states with a plantation economy. Rare was the North Carolina farm that had a slave crew totaling more than ten men and women. On North Carolina's small farms, the slaves worked in the fields side by side with the white owners. Most white farmers owned no slaves at all.

Until 1830, antislavery sentiment was strong in the Tar Heel State. About forty separate abolitionist societies (groups of men and women who wanted to end slavery) met regularly in North Carolina. One of the state's most prominent abolitionists was Lunsford Lane, a former slave who purchased his and his family's freedom and then became a powerful voice in the antislavery movement.

The attitudes of southern whites toward blacks began to harden after the 1831 rebellion led by slave Nat Turner in Virginia. Fearing a slave revolution, North Carolinians passed harsh laws concerning slaves. One law permitted local sheriffs to "visit the negroes' houses as often as may be necessary, to inflict a punishment not exceeding fifteen lashes on all slaves they may find off their owner's plantation without a proper permit or pass."

Free blacks were also affected by the hardening attitudes. After the Nat Turner Rebellion, free blacks were required to wear badges to distinguish them from slaves. Until 1835, North Carolina allowed free blacks to vote. However, the same revised 1835 constitution that gave political power to small farmers stripped away voting privileges from free blacks.

BROTHER AGAINST BROTHER

On the eve of the Civil War, North Carolina was a sharply divided state. People in the western mountains tended to be pro-Union, while the east was a Confederate stronghold. Many North Carolinians opposed slavery, but believed it was up to the individual states, not the federal government, to outlaw the practice.

Although most North Carolinians saw the issue as one of states' rights, the state did not favor secession. In fact, North Carolina seceded from the Union only after President Lincoln issued a call for troops following the attack on Fort Sumter. North Carolina was the last state to join the Confederacy. When the war began, however, most North Carolinians rallied to the southern cause. The majority agreed with future governor Jonathan Worth, who wrote, "I think the South is committing suicide, but my lot is cast with the South and being unable to manage the ship, I intend to face the breakers manfully and go down with my companions."

During the war years, the state was guided by much-beloved Governor Zebulon B. Vance. Born in the western mountains, Vance was a barrel-chested, thick-necked man blessed with a booming voice and a rollicking sense of humor. He was a vigorous supporter of states' rights and an outspoken critic of Confederate President Jefferson Davis. Though he had once been

Union troops landed at Cape Hatteras in
August 1861 (left). In December of that year,
Fort Ocracoke at the entrance to Pamlico Sound
was destroyed by Union forces (below).
According to legend, North Carolina women used
their gowns to make the regimental flag for
the Gaston Blues (above).

In 1865, a factory in Salisbury that had been converted into a military prison for captured Union soldiers was raided by Union troops that had invaded North Carolina from the west.

bitterly opposed to secession, Vance promised as governor to "prosecute the war for liberty and independence to the bitter end."

At sea, Union naval forces seized Cape Hatteras, Roanoke Island, and much of eastern North Carolina. However, the Union navy was never able to capture Wilmington, and that port city served as the "lifeline of the Confederacy." On land, a total of eighty-four battles and skirmishes were fought in North Carolina. The last battle raged at Bentonville, near Smithfield, where soldiers under the command of Union General William T. Sherman overwhelmed Confederate troops. In April 1865, Sherman marched into Raleigh. Soon afterward, the South surrendered, and the most casualty-ridden war in the nation's history came to a grim conclusion.

During the war years, North Carolina, which held one-ninth of the South's total population, furnished about one-sixth of its troops. North Carolina lost more men killed in action than any other southern state.

RECONSTRUCTION

Four years of fighting left the South humbled, war torn, and bankrupt. To readmit the southern states into the Union, Congress launched a program called Reconstruction. Many felt that some of the Reconstruction programs were designed to punish the South for its rebellion. In North Carolina, as in all the southern states, there was a short period of military rule. Then the Republicans took control of the state government. The Republican party was made up of northerners who had recently come to the South (called *carpetbaggers*), blacks, and pro-Union southern whites (called *scalawags*).

The Republicans rewrote the state constitution to include provisions that allowed all men—black or white, with or without land—to vote. Other notable provisions included the popular election of state and county officials and increased support for the education system. However, during Republican rule, many scandals occurred, public funds were wasted, and the state debt increased. Opposing the Republicans was a group that later became the Democratic party. The political infighting that ensued between the two parties included fistfights, mob action, and murder.

During the violent days of Reconstruction, the hooded secret society known as the Ku Klux Klan gained strength. Numbering almost forty thousand members in North Carolina, the Klan attacked and sometimes murdered blacks and their supporters.

In 1867, blacks in Asheville registered to vote for the first time.

Politically, the Klan backed the Democratic party. The Democrats gained control of the state legislature in 1870, and a year later they impeached and removed the Republican governor, William Holden. It was the only time in North Carolina's history that a governor was forced from office through the impeachment process.

The last political battle of the Reconstruction era was fought in 1876, when the deposed Republican William Holden ran for governor against the still-popular Civil War leader Zeb Vance. Vance won handily and cemented the power of the Democrats in the state. In the next hundred years, only one non-Democrat gained the governor's office in North Carolina.

This 1880 photograph shows workers in Coleridge pausing during the building of a dam intended to provide water for a future cotton mill.

By 1900, the Democrats had implemented a series of constitutional amendments that either limited or eliminated the gains blacks had made since emancipation. A separate school system for blacks was established. Marriages between blacks and whites were forbidden. Most importantly, an amendment required local peace officers to be appointed by the state legislature instead of being elected by the people. This made it impossible for counties with a black majority to choose their own sheriffs.

The end of Reconstruction also saw the beginning of great changes that would usher North Carolina into a new industrial era. The state government aided businesses and railroads, offering tax exemptions and commitment to industrialization. No longer could anyone think that North Carolina was asleep. The state was awake—and on the move!

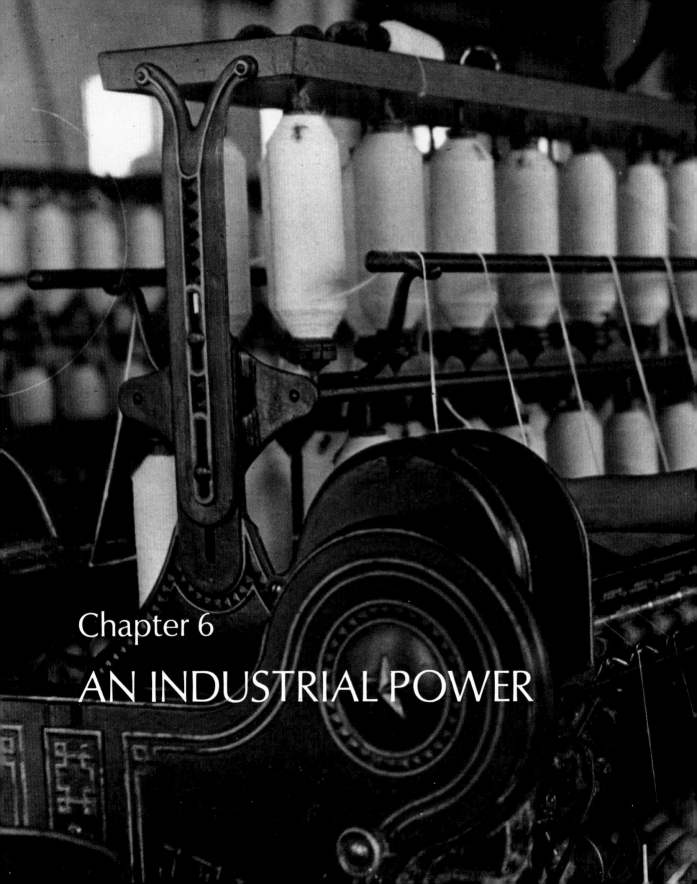

Chapter 6

AN INDUSTRIAL POWER

AN INDUSTRIAL POWER

Factories, tobacco-processing plants, and textile mills sprang up in North Carolina after the Civil War. Industrial growth revolutionized life in the once-rural Tar Heel State.

THE RISE OF INDUSTRY

Washington Duke was one of a stream of Confederate Civil War veterans who limped home after the South's defeat. When Duke arrived at his farm near present-day Durham, he had only fifty cents in his pocket, two blind mules, and a little tobacco from before the war. Duke's first tobacco harvest was a good one, and his nine-year-old son James Buchanan "Buck" Duke helped him prepare the leaves for processing. The family business soon grew into a midsize tobacco-processing plant in Durham, and Buck Duke was made a full partner when he turned eighteen.

The Duke family competed with dozens of other tobacco companies in the Durham region. One company, owned by John Ruffin Green, sold chewing tobacco in distinctive packages that featured a picture of a large black bull. Green's "Bull Durham" brand became a national bestseller. Meanwhile, Buck Duke turned his attention to the small but growing market for cigarettes. He invested in a cigarette-rolling machine that churned out 120,000 cigarettes a day. He was the first manufacturer to advertise cigarettes by putting pictures of sports stars or famous actors and actresses on the packages. In 1890, Buck Duke founded the American Tobacco Company. Soon, the company was producing

"THE FAMOUS DUKES"

HIGH GRADE
SMOKING TOBACCO

Brothers James B. and Benjamin Duke, portrayed in this 1885 tobacco advertisement (left) and in this 1920 photograph (above), dominated the nation's tobacco industry after 1900.

90 percent of all the cigarettes smoked in the United States. By 1904, Duke controlled three-fourths of the nation's tobacco industry.

The rise of the Duke tobacco empire was the most spectacular, but not the only, success story to take place in North Carolina during the post-Civil War years. One of the state's most successful businessmen was J. W. Cannon, a textile manufacturer who founded the factory town of Kannapolis. Textile mills developed in the Piedmont, where rushing rivers provided power with which to turn machinery. The Piedmont, with its fine supply of wood, also offered excellent opportunities for furniture makers. Thirty years after the war, furniture-making firms employed some two thousand North Carolina workers and earned $1.5 million in annual sales. By 1900, North Carolina was home to 7,266 factories employing more than seventy thousand workers. No other state in the South matched North Carolina's explosive business growth.

THE PERSISTENT POOR

Unfortunately, the state's spectacular gains in industry did not benefit all the state's residents. Some North Carolinians still struggled to make a living. Particularly hard hit were small farmers, industrial workers, and blacks.

The period after the Civil War saw the rise of tenant farming under the sharecropping system. Tenant farmers (also called sharecroppers) rented farmland from landowners. The tenants paid the rent by turning over a certain portion of their crop to the landowner. Rent was often as high as half or two-thirds of the year's total yield. The arrangement left the sharecropping family constantly in debt. It was nearly impossible for tenants to buy their own land. But because poor farmers had no other way to make a living, the number of North Carolina sharecroppers increased by 40 percent between 1870 and 1900. A Tarboro newspaper complained, "What demoralizes the labor of our country more than anything else is *farming on shares.*"

In 1887, an energetic farmer, Leonidas L. Polk, encouraged sharecroppers and small farmers to form a group called the Farmers' Alliance. It worked to form cooperatives so that farmers could buy and sell goods at the best possible price. Polk also started the *Progressive Farmer,* a paper that provided farmers with information on better farming techniques and urged farmers to band together to demand more support from the state government. Although the alliance began as a self-help organization, it soon aligned with a national political movement led by the Populist party. For a brief period in the 1890s, North Carolina's Populists fused with the Republicans and managed to wrest political power away from the Democrats. The Populists began feuding among themselves, however, and the party disbanded.

The board of directors of the Coleman Manufacturing Company, a black-run cotton mill that was the brainchild of Warren Coleman (seated at right)

Industrial workers in the state fared little better than the tenant farmers. Of all the state's factories, none had more brutal conditions than the cotton-textile mills. Inside the mills, the machinery clanged in a deafening roar, the work was dangerous, and the pace was furious. Women and children made up more than half of the cotton-mill work force. Labor unions, which might have pressured management to improve conditions in the factories, were unpopular in North Carolina.

Immediately following the Civil War, many blacks were impoverished, but some of the newly freed slaves enjoyed social mobility. For instance, Warren Coleman of Cabarrus County owned several businesses and eventually saved enough money to open a cotton mill that employed sixty workers. Anna Cooper, born to a slave family in Raleigh, was an influential editor and writer. Many blacks became lawyers and doctors, more than a hundred served in the state legislature during the post-Civil War years, and four were elected to the United States Congress.

The most crippling blow to black aspirations at the turn of the century was the loss of voting privileges. Most blacks were staunch supporters of the Republican party, and after that party fused with the Populists, the Democrats warned white voters of impending "Negro rule." The Democrats passed an amendment to the state constitution that, in effect, prohibited a man from voting unless his father or grandfather had been a resident voter before 1867—a period when no North Carolina black had been allowed to vote. The amendment waived this "grandfather clause" if the man could read and write. However, it was left to local white officials to judge the reading ability of a prospective voter.

The changes in voting requirements left most blacks politically powerless, and the "Jim Crow" era began in North Carolina. The term *Jim Crow*, which comes from a minstrel song, refers to the laws that formalized segregation throughout the South in the late 1800s. Under these laws, separate public facilities—such as schools, restaurants, washrooms, and seating areas on railroad cars—were required for blacks and whites. Though many of these "separate but equal" segregationist practices were time-honored southern customs, during the Jim Crow era they became laws enforceable by the state police.

PROGRESS AND THE DEPRESSION

A new era in education dawned with the election of Governor Charles B. Aycock. During Aycock's administration, from 1901 to 1905, twelve hundred schoolhouses were built, teachers' salaries were raised, the school term was lengthened, and teachers' colleges were established. Though the schools remained segregated, Aycock insisted that improvements be made in both the black and white school systems.

History was made near Kitty Hawk on December 17, 1903, when the Wright
brothers conducted the first successful powered aircraft flight.

Aviation history was made near Kitty Hawk on December 17, 1903. On that day, Orville Wright, a bicycle maker from Ohio, took to the air on a kitelike flying machine driven by a gasoline engine that was about as powerful as one of today's lawnmowers. Wright's flight lasted only twelve seconds and carried him less than half the length of a football field, but it was the first time man had left the ground in a powered, heavier-than-air machine. The amazing feat accomplished by Orville Wright and his brother Wilbur allows today's North Carolinians to boast proudly that their state is "First in Flight."

The 1920s saw great progress in communications, business, and higher education. Under Governor Cameron Morrison, who served from 1921 to 1925, more than 6,000 miles (9,656 kilometers) of roads were built at a cost of $50 million. Morrison became known as the Good Roads Governor and North Carolina earned the nickname Good Roads State. Morrison's successor,

During the Great Depression of the 1930s, federal aid helped provide medical care for people in North Carolina's rural areas.

Angus McLean, modernized state government and encouraged the growth of industry. Higher education received an enormous boost when Buck Duke donated $40 million to tiny Trinity College in Durham. The school, later renamed Duke University, became one of America's finest institutions of higher learning.

By the late 1920s, North Carolina led the states in the production of tobacco products, cotton textiles, and wooden furniture. However, the Great Depression that engulfed the nation in the 1930s brought North Carolina's business expansion to a grim halt. Farm prices dropped, factories closed, and thousands of people lost their jobs. The state and federal governments each worked to fight the depression in the Tar Heel State. The federally sponsored Civilian Conservation Corps (CCC) gave unemployed youths useful work in wilderness areas. About seventy-five thousand young North Carolinians gathered in sixty-six CCC camps to help build roads through backwoods regions and clear picnic areas in state parks. The federal government also

Members of the Women's Reserve Battalion of the United States Marine Corps take a break during their training at Camp Lejeune during World War II.

established a low-interest loan program that helped end the demoralizing system of sharecropping by allowing tenant farmers to buy the land that they worked.

WORLD WAR II AND THE POSTWAR PERIOD

During World War II, North Carolina was a teeming center of industry and agriculture. Textile products made in the state ranged from bandages to uniforms. A furniture-making firm in Mebane built 50,000 double-decker beds for the armed forces. In Wilmington, a shipbuilding company launched 126 cargo-carrying "Liberty" ships during the war years. As had been true during World War I, North Carolina was home to many military bases. Fort Bragg at Fayetteville was one of the country's largest military facilities. Camp Lejeune, which opened near Jacksonville in 1942, served the United States Marine Corps. Fighter pilots trained at the Seymour Johnson Air Force Base near Goldsboro and at the Cherry Point Marine Air Station outside Havelock.

In 1960, at a Greensboro lunch counter, four college students conducted the nation's first "sit-in."

A series of energetic governors guided the Tar Heel State through the postwar years. W. Kerr Scott, who took office in 1949, launched an ambitious "Go Forward" program to build roads and bridges and improve port facilities at Wilmington and Morehead City. Luther Hodges, who served from 1954 to 1961, was called the "Businessman's Governor" because of his campaign to attract new industries to the state. During Hodges' term, businesses invested about $1 billion for new factories and offices in North Carolina. Most important of the new projects was Research Triangle Park, a complex of laboratories and "think tanks" that was built in the late 1950s near Durham. Business expansion continued in the 1960s under Governor Terry Sanford. Sanford also brought innovative educational programs to the state, including the establishment of a state school for the performing arts and schools for gifted students. State-run community colleges and technical schools also were set up during his administration.

THE SECOND REVOLUTION

North Carolina was enjoying economic prosperity. But as in many other states, the prosperity was for "whites only." At the close of World War II, Jim Crow traditions still reigned in North Carolina, as they did in most southern states. Bus-station waiting rooms had two drinking fountains and four washrooms. Buses had a "color line" behind which all blacks had to sit. Restaurants had bold Whites Only signs above their doorways.

North Carolina civil-rights workers were among the first to introduce the "sit-in" technique to topple Jim Crow institutions. On February 1, 1960, four black college students entered the Woolworth store in Greensboro, "sat in" at the lunch counter, and announced they would not leave until they were served or dragged out by the police. Inspired by the sit-in, Greensboro's blacks began a boycott of all downtown stores, and in July, the city's lunch counters were desegregated. One of the South's most important civil-rights workers was Floyd McKissick of Asheville, who headed the organization called the Congress of Racial Equality, or CORE.

Civil-rights lawyers attacked Jim Crow practices in the federal courts. In a series of decisions, the courts struck down the "grandfather clause," literacy tests, and other devices designed to prevent blacks from voting. A landmark 1954 Supreme Court decision ruled against separate school systems for blacks and whites.

In North Carolina, school integration took place slowly, but generally without the violent protests that shook some southern states. The University of North Carolina at Chapel Hill had admitted its first black students in 1951. Two years later, black children entered previously all-white schools at Winston-Salem,

In the twentieth century, North Carolina's continuing commitment to industry was reflected in the opening in 1959 of Research Triangle Park, an industrial-research center located in the Raleigh-Durham area.

Greensboro, and Charlotte. By 1965, most of the state's school districts were integrated.

MODERN NORTH CAROLINA

In the early 1960s, the tobacco industry reacted quickly to the surgeon general's report that confirmed what doctors had long suspected: tobacco use led to lung cancer, heart disease, emphysema, and a host of other deadly diseases. The report induced millions of Americans to quit smoking. To make up for their lost sales in the United States, tobacco companies exported more of their products. Sales remained brisk, and in 1978, North Carolina's revenue from tobacco topped $1 billion for the first time in the state's history.

In the 1970s, the Republican party gained strength in North Carolina. In 1972, James E. Holshouser, Jr., became only the second Republican governor of North Carolina since

Reconstruction. That same year, Republican Jesse Helms was elected to the United States Senate. Once in office, Helms became one of Congress's most conservative members. The 1980 election of John East gave North Carolina two Republican senators for the first time in more than a hundred years.

Industry continued to expand in the 1970s and 1980s, but workers had to accept low wages. In the early 1980s, North Carolina households earned $2,000 per year less than the national average. Labor leaders accused the state government of advertising North Carolina's low wages as a lure to attract industry. Unions remain a hotly contested issue in the state. Only about 7 percent of North Carolina's workers belong to labor unions, the lowest rate of any state. Union organization is still viewed with distrust. Nevertheless, as a result of a seventeen-year organization drive, the Amalgamated Clothing and Textile Workers' Union and the J. P. Stevens textile company reached a collective-bargaining agreement. Unfortunately, the victory may be a hollow one. Many textile mills, unable to match the lower production costs abroad, have closed.

Money was no longer a worry for many factory workers who owned shares in Winston-Salem's R. J. Reynolds Tobacco Company. Due to a complicated corporate buy-out in 1988, workers discovered that their few shares of company stock suddenly were worth half a million dollars or more. Said Fred Nordenholz, president of Winston-Salem's Chamber of Commerce, "There are plenty of factory workers in bib overalls around here who are now millionaires."

Modern North Carolina is truly a land transformed. Its leaders look upon its problems as challenges to be met and goals to be achieved. In industry, agriculture, and education, North Carolina is today a leader in the family of states.

Chapter 7
GOVERNMENT AND THE ECONOMY

GOVERNMENT AND THE ECONOMY

Of all the southern states, only Texas surpasses North Carolina in factory output. In its three major industries—tobacco, textiles, and the production of wood furniture—North Carolina leads the nation. In order to function smoothly, the industries must depend on the state government to provide a favorable business climate.

GOVERNMENT

North Carolina's state government is divided into three branches: the executive, which carries out laws; the legislative, which writes new laws and rescinds old ones; and the judicial, which interprets laws and hears cases.

The executive branch is headed by the governor, who is elected to a four-year term and may be reelected only one time. The governor has wide powers. He or she appoints several important state officials, heads the budget bureau, and can call out the state militia in times of emergency. However, North Carolina is the only state that does not give the governor power to veto laws written by the state legislature. Other executive officers, all of whom are elected to four-year terms, include the lieutenant governor, attorney general, auditor, secretary of state, superintendent of public instruction, treasurer, and the commissioners of agriculture, labor, and insurance.

The legislative branch, called the General Assembly, is made up of a 50-member senate and a 120-member house of representatives. Sessions of the legislature are held yearly.

Members of the General Assembly debate proposed laws (called bills), and when a majority of the members approve, a bill becomes a law.

The highest court in the state's judicial branch is the supreme court. It has a chief justice and six associate justices. All are elected to eight-year terms. The court of appeals, the state's second-most powerful judicial body, consists of a chief judge and eleven associate judges. Appeals-court judges are also elected to eight-year terms. Lesser courts hear cases ranging from lawsuits argued by giant corporations to minor personal disputes.

Local government is administered by the boards of commissioners of the state's one hundred counties, and by officials of its many cities and towns.

The operations of state government are enormously expensive. For revenue, the state relies on an income tax, a corporation tax, a sales tax, and license fees. More than one-fourth of the state's revenue comes from federal grants.

EDUCATION

Funding the public school system is by far the largest single item in the state's budget. School expenses total more than $2 billion a year. State law requires that children between the ages of six and sixteen attend school. About 809,000 primary students and 350,000 secondary students attend North Carolina's 2,000 public schools. Today, more than half of North Carolinians over the age of eighteen are high-school graduates.

Education has long been valued in the Tar Heel State. The state's first public school opened in 1840, and by 1846 there was at least one public school in every county. Today, the state public school system sponsors exciting special programs for gifted and

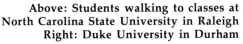

**Above: Students walking to classes at
North Carolina State University in Raleigh
Right: Duke University in Durham**

artistic students. A scholars' program, one of the first three in the
nation, allows high achievers to take advanced courses. The North
Carolina School of Science and Mathematics, the first one of its
kind in the nation, is a boarding school where gifted math and
science students work at an accelerated pace. The North Carolina
School of the Arts, also a boarding school, gives special instruction
in dance, music, painting, and sculpture.

Some of the nation's most prestigious colleges and universities
are in North Carolina. Duke University, a privately funded
institution in Durham, is famous for its medical and law schools.
Other important privately funded institutions are Davidson
College at Davidson, Meredith College at Raleigh, and Wake
Forest University at Winston-Salem.

Tobacco, shown here being picked (left) and auctioned (above), is North Carolina's leading agricultural product.

The publicly funded University of North Carolina system has sixteen campuses across the state and educates more than 120,000 students. Founded in 1795, the University of North Carolina at Chapel Hill is the nation's oldest state university. Other large institutions within the system include North Carolina State University at Raleigh, the University of North Carolina at Wilmington, the University of North Carolina at Charlotte, and the University of North Carolina at Greensboro.

AGRICULTURE

Agriculture was the Tar Heel State's principal source of income until the early 1900s. As late as 1950, agriculture was the largest source of employment in the state. Today, farmland covers about 40 percent of North Carolina, and agriculture provides about 1 percent of the state's gross product—the total value of goods and services produced in the state. About 6 percent of the state's people work on farms. Many are family members who receive no

Dairy farming is important in western North Carolina.

wages. North Carolina claims nearly seventy-three thousand farms. The average farm covers 142 acres (57 hectares).

Tobacco is the state's greatest source of farm income. Nearly 40 percent of the tobacco consumed in the United States is grown in the Tar Heel State. Though the coastal plain is famous for being a tobacco-growing center, the crop is grown in most other parts of the state as well. The town of Wilson is a leading tobacco marketplace. It sells more bright-leaf tobacco than any other city in the Western Hemisphere. A great deal of North Carolina tobacco is sold abroad.

Corn, soybeans, and peanuts are among the state's other leading crops. North Carolina grows more sweet potatoes than any other state. Fruit growers harvest apples, peaches, strawberries, and watermelons. Poultry raising is another major source of farm income. Hogs, the state's second-most important livestock product, are raised primarily in the eastern part of the state. North Carolina is the nation's number-one producer of turkeys. Beef cattle, dairy products, eggs, and ducks are other important livestock products.

NATURAL RESOURCES

North Carolina's greatest natural resource is its rich forests. About 60 percent of the state is forested. North Carolina ranks second in the nation in hardwood growing-stock, and eleventh in softwood growing-stock. The Tar Heel State ranks fourth in the nation in reserves of commercial forests. More hardwood veneer and hardwood plywood is made in North Carolina than in any other state. Of all the states, only Florida and Texas have more varieties of trees than North Carolina.

North Carolina is sometimes called Nature's Sample Case because more than three hundred different minerals and rocks are found in its soil. Rubies, sapphires, emeralds, and even diamonds have been found in the Piedmont and in the Mountain Region. Limestone is taken from mines near Charlotte, Greensboro, and Raleigh. The state ranks first in the nation in the mining of mica, and second in clay for bricks. The state also has large lithium deposits. Lithium is an important ingredient in the manufacture of aluminum and glass. Phosphate rock, used in the manufacture of fertilizers, is also mined in the state.

Along the coast, commercial fishermen haul in nearly 290 million pounds (132 million kilograms) of fish each year. More than 18,500 commercial fishing boats are licensed in the state. Leading the state's catch are shrimp, blue crab, and flounder.

MANUFACTURING

About 30 percent of the state's work force hold jobs in manufacturing. Manufacturing sales provide about 28 percent of the state's gross product. The major manufacturing centers are found in the Piedmont.

The manufacture of textiles
is North Carolina's leading
industry.

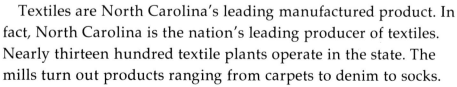

Textiles are North Carolina's leading manufactured product. In fact, North Carolina is the nation's leading producer of textiles. Nearly thirteen hundred textile plants operate in the state. The mills turn out products ranging from carpets to denim to socks.

North Carolina's Piedmont region is famous for its fine wood furniture.

Tobacco products rank second in importance among North Carolina's manufactured goods. Factories in Durham, Winston-Salem, Greensboro, and Reidsville churn out more than half of the nation's cigarettes. The state is an important producer of such chemical products as medicines and synthetic fibers. Major chemical plants stand in Raleigh, Kingston, and Shelby.

Pull up a dining-room chair in almost any home in America, and chances are that chair was made in North Carolina. Furniture making is concentrated in the Piedmont towns of Hickory, Lenoir, Lexington, Statesville, and Thomasville. High Point is such a busy furniture center that it has been called the "Furniture Capital of the United States." Other products made in North Carolina include electronic components, metalworking machinery, farm and garden machinery, and industrial equipment.

SERVICES

Service industries, which provide 65 percent of the state's gross product, employ more North Carolinians than any other enterprise. Service workers provide not products, but services for other people. Doctors, bus drivers, and supermarket baggers are all service workers. The millions of tourists who come to see the sights of the Tar Heel State are served by hotel and restaurant workers. Service industries generated by the activities at Camp Lejeune, Fort Bragg, and the Seymour Johnson Air Force Base produce hundreds of jobs for the nearby communities.

The most glamorous services are provided at Research Triangle Park, located within the triangle formed by the cities of Raleigh, Durham, and Chapel Hill. In this 5,000-acre (2,023-hectare) complex of modern buildings, scientists and engineers—working with experts from nearby Duke University, the University of North Carolina at Chapel Hill, and North Carolina State University—conduct high-level research for government and industry. It is said that Research Triangle Park has a greater concentration of men and women with doctorate degrees than any other place in the United States.

TRANSPORTATION AND COMMUNICATION

With 76,582 miles (123,243 kilometers) of roads, North Carolina has the largest state-administered highway network in the nation. Some 3,500 miles (5,633 kilometers) of railroad track cross the state. Trains still haul millions of tons of freight.

Nearly 19 million travelers are served each year at the state's thirteen major airports. The largest and busiest passenger airport is at Charlotte. In all, the state has about 350 airports.

The state's first newspaper, the *North Carolina Gazette*, was established in New Bern by James Davis in 1751. In 1799, the weekly *Raleigh Register* was founded. Today, North Carolina has 50 daily newspapers and 140 newspapers published one or more times a week. The most widely read dailies are the *Charlotte Observer* and the *News and Observer* of Raleigh. North Carolina is served by about 325 radio stations and 35 television stations.

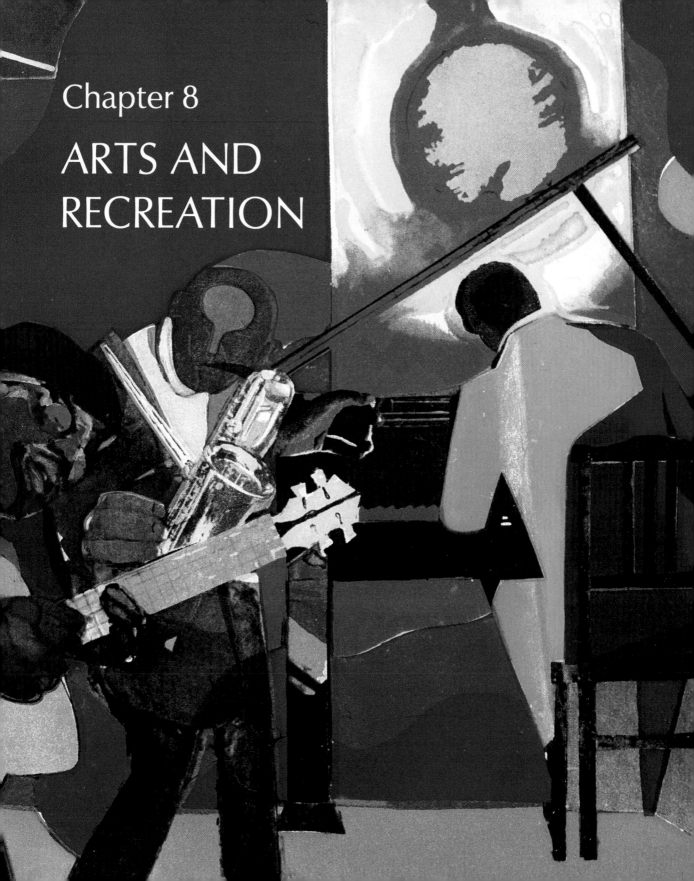

Chapter 8

ARTS AND RECREATION

ARTS AND RECREATION

In addition to thriving industries, North Carolina harbors a world of culture, sports, and leisure-time activities. It is a lively world, spiced by the creativity of the Tar Heel people.

THE ARTS

John White, the original governor of the Lost Colony, brought North Carolina to the capitals of Europe through his drawings, sketches, and paintings of the land, wildlife, and Indians of the region. Today, White's sketches serve as a valuable source of study for historians.

During the colonial era, unknown artisans created marvelous weavings, wood carvings, and furniture. Colonial women worked at looms to fashion exquisite cloth for clothes and bedcoverings, while the men made sturdy furniture, often without the use of nails.

The state's first artist of note was Elliot Daingerfield, who grew up in North Carolina after the Civil War. Daingerfield, a painter of landscapes and religious subjects, headed an art school in the Blue Ridge community of Blowing Rock. Around the same time, Mary Lyde Williams, a white artist from Duplin County, painted dramatic pictures of her black neighbors. John Barbell, a photographer from Asheville, did photographic studies of black field hands.

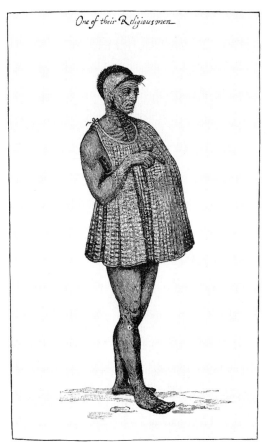

John White's sketches of North Carolina Indians, made in 1585, have served as valuable resources for historians.

During the 1920s and 1930s, organizations such as the North Carolina State Art Society were formed to promote the appreciation of art and the work of young artists. The Federal Art Project in Greensboro made a special effort to attract young blacks into the world of art. Leading artists of the period included Charles Baskerville, Jr., Donald Mattison, and Mary Tannahill.

North Carolina's art scene received its greatest boost in 1947, when Katherine P. Arrington persuaded the state legislature to appropriate $1 million to fund a state-supported museum. The North Carolina Museum of Art, which opened in 1956, is today one of the South's most prestigious museums. Among the state's other fine art museums are the William Hayes Ackland Memorial Art Center, part of the University of North Carolina at Chapel

North Carolina's noted literary figures include William Sydney Porter, who wrote under the pen name O. Henry (top left); Betty Smith (above); and Thomas Wolfe (bottom left).

Hill; and the Weatherspoon Art Gallery in Greensboro.

Contemporary Tar Heel artists whose work has been hailed by critics include Romare Bearden, Hobson Pittman, and Francis Speight.

LITERATURE

Literature in North Carolina began with a remarkable English trailblazer named John Lawson, who came to the Carolina region in 1700. Lawson's book *A New Voyage to Carolina* detailed his hikes through the rugged backwoods.

In the years just before the Civil War, Hinton Rowan Helper of Davie County attacked the institution of slavery in his book *The Impending Crisis of the South.* The book enjoyed tremendous popularity in the North but was banned in most southern states. Helper's book opposed slavery on the grounds that slavery had depressed the South's economy. A bolder antislavery book was *Walker's Appeal,* written by David Walker, a black man born in Wilmington in 1785. Another black writer in the pre-Civil War era was George Moses Horton, a slave who taught himself to read and write. Horton's collections of poetry were read and enjoyed by college students at Chapel Hill.

William Sydney Porter grew up in Greensboro shortly after the Civil War. A drifter, a gambler, and a troublemaker, he launched his writing career while languishing in a prison cell. Adopting the pen name O. Henry, Porter became one of America's most popular short-story writers. O. Henry wrote some 250 short fiction pieces, including such masterworks as "The Gift of the Magi," "The Furnished Room," and "Cabbages and Kings." Many of his stories revolve around the theme of human weakness and the influence of chance on people's lives.

Another world-renowned North Carolina writer is Thomas Wolfe, born in Asheville in 1900. In his autobiographical novel *Look Homeward, Angel,* he dramatized his dislike of the small-town shallowness and the petty jealousies displayed by his neighbors. Later, Wolfe wrote the novels *Of Time and the River, The Web and the Rock,* and *You Can't Go Home Again.* Many of his works narrate the struggles of a sensitive young man seeking value in the world but finding only corruption.

In 1943, Betty Smith, a longtime resident of Chapel Hill, published *A Tree Grows in Brooklyn.* It tells the warm and often funny story of an impoverished family struggling to survive in

New York City. *A Tree Grows in Brooklyn* is said to be one of the ten best-selling books of modern times. It has been read by people all over the world and was made into a popular movie.

North Carolina's current best-selling author is Billy Graham, whose religious books have sold millions of copies. Another contemporary North Carolina author is Alexander Key of Franklin, who wrote the young people's novel *Escape to Witch Mountain*. Humorist Harry Golden, who lived in Charlotte for many years, published a periodical called *The Carolina Israelite*.

Raleigh-born Anne Tyler has written many novels, including *Dinner at the Homesick Restaurant*, about a quirky family; and *The Accidental Tourist*, about an introverted travel writer whose life is changed when he falls in love with an unconventional dog trainer. In 1989, Tyler won the Pulitzer Prize for her novel *Breathing Lessons*.

Broadcast journalists hailing from North Carolina have made great contributions to the national news media. Edward R. Murrow, born near Greensboro, became famous for his World War II radio broadcasts, some of which were delivered from London streets during furious bombing raids. Television newsman David Brinkley was born in Wilmington, and award-winning newscaster Charles Kuralt grew up in Charlotte. Senator Jesse Helms was once a popular radio newsman for WRAL in Raleigh.

MUSIC AND THEATER

In music, North Carolina offers something for everyone. The North Carolina Symphony Orchestra, which receives funds from many of the state's corporations, plays before thousands of classical music lovers each year. A leading figure in the art of folk

The North Carolina Symphony Orchestra

music is Arthel "Doc" Watson, born in the Blue Ridge community of Deep Gap. Watson, a blind singer and guitar player, revives centuries-old mountain ballads and performs at folk festivals throughout the country. North Carolinian Earl Scruggs is one of the country's foremost bluegrass artists. Saxophonist John Coltrane, from the town of Hamlet, was a world-famous jazz musician. Perhaps the state's best-known popular singer is Roberta Flack, who was born in Black Mountain. One of Flack's best-selling recordings was "The First Time Ever I Saw Your Face," a moving song she recorded in the early 1970s.

Two kinds of music—country and gospel—command a particularly strong following in the state. Fans of country music follow such stars as Ronnie Milsap, who was born in Robbinsville; and Stonewall Jackson, who hails from Tabor. Country singer John D. Loudermilk hosted his own top-rated radio show in Durham when he was only eleven years old. One of the state's most popular gospel singers is Shirley Ceasar, who began her career as a member of a Durham-based group called the

College basketball and golf are two sports often associated with North Carolina.

Charity Sisters. The community of Kerr Lake hosts the annual Gospel Singing on the Lake.

North Carolina is known for its presentations of historical dramas, which are usually performed outside and often feature music and dancing. The "father" of such outdoor dramas is playwright Paul Green, whose most enduring work, *The Lost Colony*, has been presented on Roanoke Island every summer since 1937. It is the oldest and longest-running outdoor drama in the country. North Carolina-born actor Andy Griffith once played the part of Sir Walter Raleigh in *The Lost Colony*. The town of Snow Camp hosts the outdoor historical play *The Sword of Peace*. This drama examines a North Carolina Quaker community torn between its quest for peace and its desire to contribute to the American Revolution. Kermit Hunter is the author of *Unto These*

Hills. Performed every year in Cherokee, it dramatizes the tragedy of the Cherokee removal during the early 1800s.

SPORTS

An incredible array of sports stars were either born in the Tar Heel State or attended college there. Brothers Jim and Gaylord Perry, each of whom won the coveted Cy Young Award, were born in Williamston. Outstanding pitcher Catfish Hunter was born in Hertford. Tar Heel football players have included Charlie "Choo Choo" Justice, a star of the 1950s; and Lawrence Taylor, the fierce linebacker of the 1980s. Among the state's track champions are Dave Sime of Duke and Jim Beatty of the University of North Carolina. "Sugar Ray" Leonard, winner of more titles than any other boxer, was born in Wilmington. As for Tar Heel basketball players, that list is endless.

North Carolina did not invent the game of basketball—it only seems that way. The Big Three Colleges—Duke, the University of North Carolina at Chapel Hill, and North Carolina State—are perennial powers in the college basketball wars. Over the years, these schools have produced such legendary players as David Thompson, Bobby Jones, James Worthy, J. R. Reid, and Danny Ferry. Probably the greatest basketball player to hail from North Carolina is Michael "Air" Jordan, who grew up in Wilmington and starred at the University of North Carolina.

North Carolina's professional sports teams include the Charlotte Hornets, introduced during the 1988-89 season as an expansion team of the National Basketball Association. The minor-league Durham Bulls baseball team, which enjoys an avid following, has become even more popular since receiving attention in the movie *Bull Durham.*

Auto racing has many devoted fans in North Carolina. The Charlotte Motor Speedway hosts such championship races as the World 600 and the Mellow Yellow 300. A popular event in Wilkes County is the Wilkes Grand National Stock Race. Famed race-car driver Richard Petty, a native North Carolinian, was elected to the state's Sports Hall of Fame in 1973.

The charming village of Pinehurst is a mecca for golf enthusiasts. Two dozen lush, green golf courses dot the land within a 20-mile (32-kilometer) radius of the village center. A place where celebrities often play, Pinehurst is also the home of the World Golf Hall of Fame.

FAIRS AND FUN

On any given weekend, a community somewhere in North Carolina is holding a fair, festival, or some sort of celebration. Farming towns celebrate planting seasons or harvests with such events as Chadbourn's Strawberry Festival or Clayton's North Carolina Soybean Festival. History is the theme of Dare Days, celebrated at Manteo, not far from the birthplace of Virginia Dare. During Denim Fun Days, a citywide party in Erwin, everyone wears the comfortable fabric in honor of the area's numerous denim-producing textile mills.

Music and arts and crafts serve as themes for many fairs held in the state. Black Mountain hosts a popular bluegrass festival. Union Grove sponsors the Old Time Fiddlers' Convention. Square dancing is featured at Asheville's Shindig on the Green. Arts and handcrafts are displayed at Wilson's Sunday in the Park Festival. The fine arts are honored at Wilmington's St. Thomas Celebration of the Arts. North Carolinians celebrate the heritage of their ancestors during events such as the Highland Games and Scottish

Above: The Blue Ridge Folk
Art Center near Asheville
Top right: A Civil War
reenactment in Raleigh
Bottom right: A folk festival
in the Blue Ridge Mountains

Clan Gathering at Grandfather Mountain and Moravian Easter
services in Old Salem.

Of course, an old-fashioned festival in North Carolina need not
have a serious theme. Instead of a beauty pageant, the town of
Clinton presents the Eastern North Carolina Ugly Pick-up Truck
Contest. Loudmouths gather at Spivey's Corner near Fayetteville
for the National Hollerin' Contest. Benson has Mule Day
Celebration, and Saluda puts on a Coon Dog Barking Contest.
Lizard races are held, appropriately enough, at Lizard Lick.

Chapter 9

A TAR HEEL TOUR

A TAR HEEL TOUR

North Carolina's twenty-eight state parks, four national forests, and the Great Smoky Mountains National Park contain outdoor adventures for everyone. The cities boast museums, libraries, and architectural surprises. North Carolina has experienced four centuries of American history, and the past is always present in the form of historic buildings and sites. It would take a lifetime to see all that North Carolina has to offer, but a quick tour beginning at the Atlantic Coast and ending in the Blue Ridge Mountains provides at least a taste of the Tar Heel State.

THE OUTER BANKS

The Outer Banks consist of the sandbars and many islands that lie off the state's seacoast. Seaside walks are popular at Cape Hatteras National Seashore, a 30,000-acre (12,141-hectare) preserve. In 1958, Hatteras became the first coastal park in the nation to be given national seashore status. Today, nearly the entire chain that makes up the northern Outer Banks is national seashore.

Situated near Kitty Hawk and Kill Devil Hills is a tall stone monument to the Wright brothers. Almost a century ago, the world's first powered airplane flight took place on these historic grounds. The Wright brothers chose to conduct their aerial experiments at Kill Devil Hills because the National Weather

The world's first powered aircraft flight is commemorated at the Wright Brothers National Memorial near Kill Devil Hills.

Service had informed them that it was one of the windiest regions in North America.

Nags Head Woods in the north Outer Banks is a protected region of wetlands and hardwood forests that still looks much as it did when early white settlers arrived. Jockey's Ridge State Park is a nature area that boasts the largest sand dune in eastern North America. Hang-gliding enthusiasts dash down this dune in order to gather speed and take off on their dizzying flights. The nearby Pea Island National Wildlife Refuge is the winter home for flocks of greater snow geese and dozens of other species.

History comes alive at Roanoke Island, where, some four hundred years ago, the members of the first English colony in North America struggled to survive. Museum displays at Fort Raleigh describe the trials and perils of the English settlers who landed on this spot in the 1580s. Every year, thousands come to Roanoke to watch the outdoor play *The Lost Colony*.

Above: Windsurfing off Cape Hatteras
Right: Fishing boats at Ocracoke Island

Among the highlights of the Outer Banks are the graceful old lighthouses that stand like silent sentinels gazing over the Atlantic. Cape Hatteras Lighthouse, built in 1870, towers 208 feet (63 meters) above the sand dunes, making it America's tallest brick lighthouse. To the south stands Bald Head Lighthouse, built in 1817. No longer do these structures warn vessels away from dangerous shoals. Instead, they rise as mute symbols of the time when the treacherous waters of the Outer Banks struck terror in the hearts of sailors.

North Carolina's southern islands have many popular swimming beaches, such as those located at Topsail Island and at Hammocks Beach State Park. Airlie Gardens at Wrightsville Beach dazzles visitors with its display of azaleas and camellias. In the Cape Fear region is Fort Fisher State Historic Site, the site of a Civil War fortress that once protected the city of Wilmington.

Island-hopping in the Outer Banks is bound to work up an appetite, and the North Carolina coast has long been famous for its fine seafood restaurants. The tiny coastal village of Calabash has a population of only about two hundred, but it has twenty-

two restaurants specializing in seafood delicacies. As far away as
New York City, seafood lovers speak longingly of fried fish done
"Calabash style."

THE ATLANTIC COASTAL PLAIN

The northeast corner of the Atlantic Coastal Plain is known as
the "Cradle of North Carolina." The town of Bath, incorporated in
1705, is North Carolina's oldest town. Historic Edenton is a
treasure trove of eighteenth-century architecture. Construction on
Edenton's charming St. Paul's Church began in 1736. The town's
Chowan County Courthouse, built in 1767, is described as "one of
the most distinguished eighteenth-century buildings in the
South." The history of the Cradle of North Carolina can be
studied at the Albemarle Museum in Elizabeth City.

To the northwest is Roanoke Rapids, a town founded as a
cotton-mill center in 1893. The fishing at the nearby city of
Weldon is so good that the town calls itself the "Rockfish Capital
of the World." In Rocky Mount stands a fascinating children's
museum devoted to the natural sciences. Tarboro, incorporated in
1760, has many splendid old homes and is one of the most
beautiful communities in the state. In the town of Kenly, the
Tobacco Museum of North Carolina displays the history of the
state's most important cash crop. Fayetteville has many historic
buildings, including the old Market House, which stands on the
site of the building where North Carolina delegates ratified the
United States Constitution in 1789.

Spreading along the coast is the Croatan National Forest, a vast
woodland laced with hiking trails. The ports of Morehead City
and Beaufort lie east of the forest. In Beaufort, the North Carolina
Maritime Museum holds an impressive collection of ship models

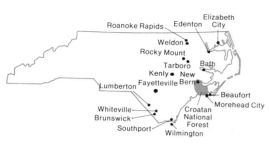

Visitors may wander through magnificent eighteenth-century-style gardens at Tryon Palace in New Bern.

and exhibits on coastal birds. Walking the streets of New Bern, a visitor can find more than 150 landmarks listed on the National Register of Historic Places. New Bern's Tryon Palace, built in 1767 as the office and residence of Royal Governor William Tryon, has been magnificently restored and is open to the public. Before the Revolutionary War, Tryon Palace was considered one of the most beautiful public buildings in all colonial America. After the war, it was used as North Carolina's first state capitol.

Wilmington, rich in history, is one of the state's most fascinating cities. Elegant buildings abound in Wilmington, including the Burgwin-Wright House, built in 1770; and Thalian Hall, a beautifully restored nineteenth-century theater. The Wilmington Railroad Museum presents the story of railroading during the city's heyday as a southern port. The New Hanover County Museum is dedicated to regional history. Another popular Wilmington attraction is the retired battleship USS *North Carolina*, anchored permanently at the city's riverfront. Completed in 1939, this monster warship took part in some of World War II's most furious sea battles.

Greenfield Gardens in Wilmington

Near Wilmington lies a host of interesting places to visit. Brunswick, a colonial seaport that was burned by the British in 1776, is now a state historic site. The coastal village of Southport, whose roots date back to 1754, has the look and charm of a New England fishing village. Orton Plantation, once the headquarters of a rice empire, includes an avenue of enormous live oaks and magnificent gardens filled with brilliant patches of azaleas, roses, and camellias. North of Wilmington is Moores Creek National Military Park. There, in 1776, North Carolina patriots defeated British loyalists in the first Revolutionary War battle fought in North Carolina.

Wilderness areas are a delightful feature of the southern coastal plain. Lake Waccamaw State Park awes visitors with its huge lake surrounded by graceful cypress trees. Singletary Lake State Park, east of Elizabethtown, is a 1,200-acre (486-hectare) recreation area. The nearby city of Lumberton was once — true to its name — a trading center for logs and other forest products.

Raleigh, North Carolina's capital, is also one of the state's most populous cities.

THE NORTHERN PIEDMONT

The northern half of the Piedmont is the state's most populous region. Cities there are strung like necklace beads along highways I-85 and I-40. Although the northern Piedmont is the industrial heartland of the state, it also includes many wilderness areas that harbor breathtaking natural beauty.

Raleigh, the state capital, offers the visitor many museums and historical sites. The North Carolina Museum of History tells the epic story of the state through films, dioramas, and soundtracks. Plants and animals native to the Tar Heel State are featured in the North Carolina Museum of Natural History. The North Carolina Museum of Art contains eighteenth- and nineteenth-century masterpieces. Its Egyptian artifact collection is perhaps the best in the South. Architecture buffs appreciate the Victorian lines of the Governor's Mansion, located a short distance from the state capitol.

Chapel Hill, home of the University of North Carolina, is also home to the Ackland Art Museum, which houses a collection of international art. The North Carolina Botanical Gardens, a 307-acre (124-hectare) park filled with rare herbs and plants, is another Chapel Hill attraction. The city's Morehead Planetarium allows spectators to follow the passage of stars through the night sky.

The city of Durham dates to the 1850s, making it young by North Carolina standards. The Duke family tobacco empire stirred the city's industrial growth. For many years, black-owned businesses have contributed to Durham's progress as well. Until World War II, the headquarters of the North Carolina Mutual Life Insurance Company—an entirely black-owned firm—was the city's tallest building. Visitors to today's Durham tour the lovely campus of Duke University and view exhibits at the North Carolina Museum of Life and Science.

West of Durham on Interstate 85 is historic Hillsborough, founded in the 1750s by Scotch-Irish settlers. For a brief period during the American Revolution, the General Assembly met here.

The city of Burlington is a bargain-hunter's delight, with more than a hundred factory-outlet clothing stores. Near Burlington is the Alamance Battlefield, where two thousand Piedmont frontiersmen, known as the Regulators, battled the colonial militia in 1771. The highlight of Reidsville is the lush, twenty-seven-room Plantation Home, built in the 1920s by a tobacco tycoon. The mansion has exquisite furniture and artwork collected from every corner of the world.

Indian and pioneer relics are displayed at the Greensboro Historical Museum. Also in Greensboro is the Natural Science Center. To the south is Asheboro, site of the 1,300-acre (526-hectare) North Carolina Zoological Park.

The towns of Winston and Salem grew as separate communities until they merged in 1913. Winston-Salem has been a major tobacco center since cigarette magnate R. J. Reynolds opened a tobacco factory there more than a hundred years ago. Visitors

Historic Old Salem includes restorations of the businesses (above) and homes (right) of the Moravians who founded the town in the 1700s.

flock to the city's famous art museums: the Museum of Early Southern Decorative Arts, where arts and crafts of the colonial South are displayed; and the Southeastern Center for Contemporary Art, which holds modern paintings and sculptures. Historic Old Salem, a village within the city, allows visitors to take a leisurely walk into the past and view the lifestyle of Salem's early Moravian settlers.

Factories in the city of High Point turn out tons of furniture each year. Appropriately, pieces of antique furniture are among the articles displayed at the High Point Museum and Historical Park. South of High Point is Salisbury, which features a twenty-three-block section of historic homes.

Rugged mountains and rolling hills rise in the northern Piedmont. Hanging Rock State Park challenges amateur mountain climbers to scale its stark cliffs and capture breathtaking views.

Nearby Pilot Mountain State Park has a spectacular quartzite rock formation that climbs 1,500 feet (457 meters) into the sky.

THE SOUTHERN PIEDMONT

The southern Piedmont town of Rockingham is a historic community. Founded in 1875, it was named after the Marquis of Rockingham, an English nobleman. Racing fans know Rockingham as the host city for a popular stock-car race. At Waxhaw, near the city of Monroe, the powerful outdoor drama *Listen and Remember* is presented. The play explores the lives of early North Carolina pioneers, including the parents of Andrew Jackson. To the north is a reconstruction of the Reed Gold Mine, where Conrad Reed stumbled upon gold in 1799. The mine serves as a reminder that North Carolina was the nation's biggest gold producer until the 1848 strike in California.

Near Albemarle is Morrow Mountain State Park, a vast facility where visitors can hike, camp, or participate in organized nature studies. South of the park spreads the huge Uwharrie National Forest—46,000 acres (18,616 hectares) of wooded mountains sprawling over three counties. On the southern fringe of the forest is the Town Creek Indian Mound State Historic Site, where visitors may tour a reconstructed Indian ceremonial center.

Charlotte, North Carolina's largest city, has both downtown glass-and-steel towers that symbolize the new, and quiet side-street neighborhoods that reflect the charm of the Old South. A popular site near Charlotte is Latta Place, a home built in 1799 by James Latta, one of the southern Piedmont's most successful farmers. Another charming relic of the past is the Hezekiah Alexander home, a 1774 farmhouse now recognized as the oldest dwelling still standing in the Charlotte region.

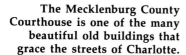

The Mecklenburg County Courthouse is one of the many beautiful old buildings that grace the streets of Charlotte.

The first branch of the United States Mint was built in Charlotte in 1845, and the original building, moved to a new site, now serves as the Mint Museum of Art. North Carolina's largest museum of science and technology is Charlotte's Discovery Place, where visitors enjoy many hands-on exhibits. Live animals and the Nature Trail are features of the city's Nature Museum.

In the Charlotte area are many other places of interest. To the north is man-made Lake Norman, the state's largest lake and an outstanding place to fish. The city of Kannapolis, the headquarters of the once-mighty Cannon Textile Company, is now a maze of factory-outlet stores that draw bargain hunters from around the country. At the Charlotte Motor Speedway is the Museum of Fine Motor Cars, where many classic automobiles are displayed. South of the city is Carowinds, a theme park that features rides, shows, and historical attractions. Nearby is the birthplace of James K. Polk, one of three American presidents born in North Carolina.

The James K. Polk Memorial is a re-creation of the farm where the eleventh president spent some of his boyhood years.

Driving east toward the Blue Ridge Mountains, many tourists stop at the town of Belmont to see the Belmont Abbey Church, a graceful structure completed in 1894. At Gastonia is the Schiele Museum of Natural History and Planetarium, which includes a re-creation of a North Carolina pioneer village. More than ninety species of birds nest at nearby Crowder's Mountain State Park.

At the town of Shelby is the Cleveland County Historical Museum, where lectures and art festivals are presented. Though the village of McAdenville has fewer than a thousand people, it is known throughout the state for the glorious light displays put up by its citizens during the holiday season. Residents call McAdenville the Christmas Town.

THE MOUNTAIN REGION

The Blue Ridge region and its adjoining high country contain some of the most spellbinding mountain scenery in the United

The famous mile-high swinging bridge at Grandfather Mountain

States. This western end of North Carolina is often called the "Land of the Sky."

Stone Mountain State Park, near the town of Boone, contains more than 11,000 acres (4,452 hectares) of untamed forests spreading over a rugged mountain range. The lush woodlands of the New River country lie to the north. Despite its name, geologists believe that the New River is older than the Nile. Threading through the wonders of this mountain country is the Blue Ridge Parkway. This highway, a sightseer's delight, stretches nearly 250 miles (402 kilometers) through the scenic heart of the Land of the Sky.

Near the town of Linville rises Grandfather Mountain, so named because its peak looks like the face of an old man lost in sleep. Tourists at Grandfather Mountain may cross a mile-high (1.6-kilometer-high) swinging bridge that connects two crests. The Pisgah National Forest—more than a million acres (404,690 hectares) of woodland—attracts hikers and campers. Linville Falls is a two-step cascade that thrills visitors with its surging power. Nearby Linville Caverns is an underground fairyland of stalactites and stalagmites.

Reconstructed pioneer cabins at the Great Smoky Mountains National Park

The Museum of North Carolina Minerals, located near the town of Spruce Pine, exhibits more than three hundred kinds of minerals and gems found in the Tar Heel State. Burnsville is the home of the Parkway Playhouse, where professional actors work with university students to produce summer theater works. Winter sports enthusiasts come to such towns as Blowing Rock, Banner Elk, and Boone to ski the nearby slopes.

Great Smoky Mountains National Park is the scenic gem of the Land of the Sky. Spilling into Tennessee, the parkland covers more than 500,000 acres (202,345 hectares) and contains 600 miles (966 kilometers) of bubbling mountain streams. The Great Smoky Mountains earned their name from the smoky mist that often covers their peaks. The Appalachian Trail—a scenic hiking path that extends through fourteen states from Maine to Georgia and runs for 200 miles (322 kilometers) in North Carolina alone—winds through the Great Smoky Mountains National Park.

South of the park is the Qualla Cherokee Indian Boundary, home of the Eastern Band of the Cherokee Nation. The Cherokee are the only original North Carolinians who retain a tribal

The French-Renaissance-style Biltmore House in Asheville

identity within the state. At the town of Cherokee stands a reconstructed Cherokee village and a museum devoted to the nation's history and culture.

At Asheville is the elegant Biltmore Estate. The centerpiece of the 12,000-acre (4,856-hectare) estate is the Biltmore House, a masterpiece of French Renaissance architecture. The mansion, once owned by the Vanderbilt family, has 250 rooms and is said to be the world's largest private home.

At the town of Lake Lure is Chimney Rock, an amazing geological formation that towers high above the neighboring mountains. To the west is "Waterfall Country," where cascades such as Bridal Veil Falls, Connestee Falls, and Whitewater Falls work their magic. Summer theater thrives at the town of Flat Rock, which supports the Flat Rock Playhouse.

In the western part of the Blue Ridge region, mountain peaks pierce the sky like heavenly cathedral spires. Whiteside Mountain near the town of Highlands boasts the highest sheer cliffs in the eastern United States. The Nantahala National Forest is a

View from the Blue Ridge Parkway near Glendale Springs

wilderness collage of rugged mountains and stately woodlands. The view into the spectacular Nantahala Gorge, which plunges deep into the earth, is so awesome that ancient Indians believed it was haunted.

The majestic Blue Ridge Mountains are a perfect place to end a tour of North Carolina. From its seacoast to its mountains, North Carolina is a state unsurpassed for beauty and excitement.

The Tar Heel State is also sometimes called the Old North State. The state has an official toast that people sometimes recite with raised glasses:

> Here's to the land of the long-leaf pine,
> The summer land where the sun doth shine,
> Where the weak grow strong and the strong grow great,
> Here's to "Down Home" the Old North State!

107

FACTS AT A GLANCE

GENERAL INFORMATION

Statehood: November 21, 1789, twelfth state

Origin of Name: In 1629, the huge tract of land that included what would become North Carolina and South Carolina was named *Carolana* (the Latin form of Charles) in honor of King Charles I of England. The spelling was later changed to *Carolina*. North Carolina and South Carolina became separate colonies in 1712.

State Capital: Raleigh, founded in 1792

State Nicknames: Tar Heel State and Old North State

State Flag: North Carolina's state flag was adopted in 1885. The left third of the flag is a vertical blue stripe. The right two-thirds is divided into one red and one white horizontal stripe. On the blue stripe are the gold letters "NC" and a white star. Two dates in black letters appear on golden scrolls. The top date, May 20, 1775, marks the "Mecklenburg Declaration of Independence," which proclaimed Mecklenburg County's independence from England. The bottom date, April 12, 1776, was the day that North Carolina's Continental Congress delegates were instructed to vote for independence.

State Motto: *Esse Quam Videri*, "To Be Rather Than To Seem"

State Bird: Cardinal

State Mammal: Gray squirrel

State Flower: Flowering dogwood

State Tree: Pine

State Gem Stone: Emerald

State Insect: Honeybee

State Reptile: Turtle

State Shell: Scotch bonnet

State Colors: Red and blue

State Song: "The Old North State," adopted in 1927, words by William Gaston and music by Mrs. E. E. Randolph:

Carolina! Carolina! heaven's blessings attend her,
While we live we will cherish, protect, and defend her,
Tho' the scorner may sneer at and witlings defame her,
Still our hearts swell with gladness when ever we name her.

Chorus:
Hurrah! Hurrah! the Old North State forever,
Hurrah! Hurrah! The good Old North State.

Tho' she envies not others their merited glory,
Gay whose name stands the foremost, in liberty's story,
Tho' too true to her self e'er to crouch to oppression,
Who can yield to just rule a more loyal submission.

(Chorus)

Then let all those who love us love the land that we live in,
As happy a region as on this side of heaven.
Where plenty and peace, love and joy smile before us,
Raise aloud, raise together the heart-thrilling chorus.

(Chorus)

POPULATION

Population: 5,881,813, tenth among the states (1980 census)

Population Density: 112.4 people per sq. mi. (43 people per km²)

Population Distribution: 48 percent of North Carolina residents live in cities or towns.

Charlotte	314,447
Greensboro	155,642
Raleigh	150,255
Winston-Salem	131,885
Durham	100,538
High Point	63,808
Fayetteville	59,507
Asheville	53,583
Gastonia	47,333
Wilmington	44,000
Rocky Mount	41,283

(Population figures according to 1980 census)

Population Growth: North Carolina has shown steady population growth since statehood. In recent years it has been one of the fastest growing states in the South. Newcomers have entered North Carolina for its pleasant weather, favorable business climate, topflight universities, and relaxed lifestyle. The fastest-growing section of the state is the "Research Triangle" in the Raleigh-Durham area.

Year	Population
1790	393,751
1800	478,103
1820	638,839
1840	753,419
1860	992,622
1880	1,399,750
1900	1,893,810
1920	2,559,123
1940	3,571,623
1950	4,061,929
1960	4,556,155
1970	5,084,411
1980	5,881,813

GEOGRAPHY

Borders: North Carolina is bounded by Virginia on the north, Tennessee on the west, Georgia and South Carolina on the south, and the Atlantic Ocean on the east and southeast.

Highest Point: Mount Mitchell, 6,684 ft. (2,037 m)

Lowest Point: Sea level, at the Atlantic Ocean

Greatest Distances: North to south—187 mi. (301 km)
East to west—503 mi. (809 km)

Area: 52,669 sq. mi. (136,413 km²)

Rank in Area Among the States: Twenty-eighth

National Forests and Parklands: The Great Smoky Mountains National Park, covering lands in both North Carolina and Tennessee, is America's most frequently visited national park. Cape Hatteras National Seashore on the Outer Banks has about 70 mi. (113 km) of beach. Another protected land, Cape Lookout National Seashore, extends for 60 mi. (97 km). North Carolina has four national forests: Croatan on the coastal plain, Uwharrie in the Piedmont, and Pisgah and Nantahala in the western mountains. Moores Creek near Wilmington and Guilford Courthouse near Greensboro are national military parks.

Lake Norman is the largest man-made lake lying wholly within North Carolina.

Rivers: North Carolina's rivers may be divided into three groups. Rivers such as the Cape Fear, Roanoke, Neuse, and Tar-Pamlico start in the Piedmont and flow south and southeast through the Atlantic Coastal Plain. The Yadkin-Pee Dee, Catawba, and Broad flow through the Piedmont and into South Carolina or Georgia. The rivers of the third group originate in the Blue Ridge and flow into Tennessee. These include the French Broad, Little Tennessee, Hiwassee, and Wataugua rivers.

Lakes: Most of North Carolina's natural lakes lie on the coastal plain. The largest, Lake Mattamuskeet, covers 67 sq. mi. (174 km²). Other natural lakes include Waccamaw, Phelps, Pungo, and Alligator. Most of North Carolina's large lakes are man-made reservoirs. Lake Norman on the Catawba River is the largest artificial lake lying wholly within the state, followed by Fontana Lake on the Little Tennessee River. John Kerr Reservoir and Roanoke Rapids Reservoir, both on the Roanoke River, are shared with Virginia.

Cape Lookout National Seashore

Coast: North Carolina's coastline extends 301 mi. (484 km) from the Virginia border to the South Carolina border. However, including sandbars, islands, bays, and the mouths of rivers, the shoreline runs 3,375 mi. (5,432 km). The sandbars off the coast have formed a long barrier known as the Outer Banks. These banks created Cape Hatteras, Cape Lookout, and Cape Fear. Cape Hatteras is called the Graveyard of the Atlantic because its shifting sands have caused many shipwrecks.

Topography: North Carolina contains three major land regions. The eastern flatland, part of the Atlantic Coastal Plain, covers two-fifths of the state. It extends from the ocean inland to the Fall Line, where soft coastal soil ends and rocky hill country begins. Swamps, savannahs, and natural lakes dot the fertile farmland of this region.

The Piedmont, a gently rolling plateau, extends through the center of the state. Many narrow, swift streams flow through the red clay of this region. Most of North Carolina's people live here.

Western North Carolina contains the Mountain Region. This is part of the larger Appalachian mountain system. The rugged area includes the Blue Ridge, Great Smoky, and other mountain ranges. Mount Mitchell lies in the Black Mountains, near Asheville. At 6,684 ft. (2,037 m), it is the highest peak in the eastern United States.

A red-winged blackbird in the Dismal Swamp

Climate: The plains, hills, and mountains of North Carolina provide the state with a range of climates. At Wilmington, on the coastal plain, temperatures average 46.5° F. (8° C) in January and 70° F. (21° C) in July. Charlotte, in the Piedmont, sees average January temperatures of 43° F. (6° C) in January and 79° F. (26° C) in July. Mountainous Asheville has January temperatures of 35° F. (2° C) in January and 72° F. (22° C) in July. The coastal plain receives about 50 in. (127 cm) of precipitation annually. About 47 in. (119 cm) fall on the Piedmont. The Mountain Region receives about 60 in. (152 cm), including about 40 in. (102 cm) of snow. The state's weather extremes include a highest recorded temperature of 109° F. (43° C) at Albemarle on July 28, 1940. The lowest temperature on record was -29° F. (-34° C) at Mount Mitchell on January 30, 1966. The state's generally temperate weather is occasionally interrupted by violent storms. Tornados occasionally sweep through inland areas and hurricanes are an almost yearly hazard along the coast.

NATURE

Trees: Spruces, balsams, palmettos, wild olives, cedars, cypresses, gum hickories, maples, oaks, pine tulips, tupelos, ashes, longleaf pines

Wild Plants: Rhododendrons, mountain laurels, sumacs, azaleas, Venus's-flytraps, dogwoods, camellias, redbuds, orchids, pitcher plants, sundews

Animals: Black bears, deer, foxes, beavers, squirrels, opossums, raccoons, rabbits, otters, skunks, mink, dolphins, oysters, clams, shrimp, turtles, rattlesnakes, copperheads, coral snakes, water moccasins

Birds: Quail, ruffed grouse, wild turkeys, cardinals, wrens, mockingbirds, chickadees, woodpeckers, warblers, mourning doves, partridges, woodcocks

Fish: Marlin, menhaden, sailfish, sturgeon, bluefish, weakfish, croaker, bass, bluegill, crappie, sunfish, trout, shad

The General Assembly, which originally met in the State Capitol (above), now holds its sessions in the specially built Legislative Building.

GOVERNMENT

North Carolina's government, like the federal government, is divided into legislative, executive, and judicial branches. The legislature, called the General Assembly, makes laws. It is composed of a 50-member senate elected from 35 districts and a 120-member house of representatives elected from 72 districts. All legislators serve two-year terms.

The governor heads the executive branch. He or she enforces the state's laws. But North Carolina's governor, unlike those of other states, cannot veto a bill passed by the legislature. Other executive officials include the lieutenant governor, secretary of state, treasurer, superintendent of public instruction, attorney general, auditor, commissioner of agriculture, commissioner of labor, and commissioner of insurance. All officials are elected to four-year terms. The governor and lieutenant governor may serve only two terms.

North Carolina's supreme court has a chief justice and six associate justices. The court of appeals has twelve justices. The superior court has sixty-six justices. All are elected to eight-year terms. District-court judges rule on minor cases. They are elected to four-year terms. The governor appoints a successor to any justice who leaves office during his or her term.

Number of Counties: 100

U.S. Representatives: 11

Electoral Votes: 13

The University of
North Carolina
at Chapel Hill is
the nation's oldest
state university.

EDUCATION

North Carolina law requires that all children between the ages of six and sixteen attend school. The state's elementary and secondary public school system includes about 2,000 schools with an enrollment of about 1.3 million students.

The University of North Carolina, founded in 1795, is the oldest state university in America. It now has sixteen campuses, including Chapel Hill, Raleigh (North Carolina State University), Greensboro, Charlotte, Asheville, and Wilmington. Duke University in Durham, Wake Forest University in Winston-Salem, and Davidson College in Davidson are outstanding private institutions. Other colleges and universities include Atlantic Christian College in Wilson; Barber-Scotia College in Concord; Belmont Abbey College in Belmont; Campbell University in Buies Creek; Catawba College in Salisbury; Elon College in Elon College; Gardner-Webb College in Boiling Springs; Greensboro College and Guilford College, both in Greensboro; High Point College in High Point; Lenoir-Rhyne College in Hickory; Livingstone College in Salisbury; Mars Hill College in Mars Hill; Meredith College, St. Augustine's College, and Shaw University, all in Raleigh; Methodist College in Fayetteville; North Carolina Wesleyan College in Rocky Mount; Pfeiffer College in Misenheimer; Queens College in Charlotte; St. Andrews Presbyterian College in Laurinburg; Salem College in Winston-Salem; Southeastern Baptist Theological Seminary in Wake Forest; Warren Wilson College in Swannanoa; and Wingate College in Wingate.

ECONOMY AND INDUSTRY

Principal Products:

Agriculture: Tobacco, corn, soybeans, peanuts, sweet potatoes, apples, peaches, strawberries, watermelons, poultry, hogs, turkeys, eggs, dairy products, beef cattle

Manufacturing: Textiles, tobacco products, chemicals, wood and paper products, clothing, electric equipment, metal products, furniture, leather products

Natural Resources: Forests, limestone, phosphate, sand and gravel, clays, mica, lithium, asbestos, feldspar, olivine, tungsten, fish

Business: Service industries account for most of North Carolina's business, forming 65 percent of the gross state product. Wholesale and retail trade account for 18 percent. Government makes up another 13 percent. Finance, insurance, real estate, social services, transportation, communications, and utilities contribute another 34 percent.

North Carolina is the Southeast's leading manufacturing state. Manufacturing accounts for 28 percent of the state's gross product. Textiles are North Carolina's most important product. North Carolina leads the nation in textile production. North Carolina also leads the states in the production of tobacco products and household furniture.

Agriculture was once the state's most important source of income. Today, it accounts for 1 percent of the gross state product. Tobacco, broilers, hogs, peanuts, dairy products, corn, and soybeans are important products. North Carolina leads the nation in sweet potato production.

Charlotte and Raleigh are major wholesale trade centers. Asheville is a regional wholesale trade center. Modern ports at Wilmington and Morehead City ship North Carolina's textiles, tobacco products, and furniture throughout the world.

Communication: Many of North Carolina's largest newspapers are more than a century old. The leading daily newspapers are the *Charlotte Observer* and the *News and Observer* of Raleigh. There are about 190 newspapers in North Carolina, including about 50 dailies.

The state's oldest radio station, WBT, began broadcasting in Charlotte in 1922. WBTV of Charlotte and WFMY of Greensboro, established in 1949, were North Carolina's first television stations. North Carolina has about 325 radio stations and about 35 television stations.

Transportation: Rivers and Indian paths served as the first North Carolina routes. Although many of the region's rivers were navigable, few had good outlets for ocean trade. The state's road-building efforts, which began in the 1850s, proved so successful that North Carolina became known as the Good Roads State. North Carolina has about 76,582 mi. (123,243 km) of roads. Six interstate highways cross the state.

The state's first major railroad, the Wilmington and Raleigh, was completed in 1840. At one time, the 161-mi. (259-km) Wilmington railroad was the longest in the world. Today, some 3,500 mi. (5,633 km) of railroad track cross the state.

Seven commercial airlines serve the state at about 350 airports. Morehead City, Southport, and Wilmington have harbors that are part of the Atlantic Intracoastal Waterway.

Bogue Sound near Morehead City

SOCIAL AND CULTURAL LIFE

Museums: The North Carolina Museum of Art in Raleigh is considered one of the finest art museums in the South. The Mint Museum of Art in Charlotte displays European and American paintings. Chinese porcelains and traditional American art may be found at the Hickory Museum of Art in Hickory. Winston-Salem's Museum of Early Southern Decorative Arts features regional crafts. Other art museums include the Weatherspoon Art Gallery in Greensboro and the Reynolds House in Winston-Salem.

The North Carolina Museum of Life and Science has extensive natural-history exhibits. The Charlotte Nature Museum is a children's museum. At the University of North Carolina at Chapel Hill is Morehead Planetarium, one of the nation's oldest and best-known planetariums. The North Carolina Maritime Museum in Beaufort contains natural-history and maritime exhibits.

The state has many museums that display historical items. The North Carolina Museum of History in Raleigh chronicles the history of the state. The Greensboro Historical Museum contains relics from seven wars. The Museum of the Cherokee Indian has the largest and finest collection of Cherokee artifacts and relics in the eastern United States.

Libraries: North Carolina's first public library opened in Bath in 1700. The state's first tax-supported public library opened in 1897. Today, public libraries serve all counties, through local libraries and bookmobiles.

North Carolina has more than ninety college and university libraries. Duke University's library has about 3.6 million volumes. The library at the University of North Carolina at Chapel Hill houses some 3.5 million volumes. Both libraries are well known for their southern-history and social-science collections.

Hang gliding at Nags Head in the Outer Banks

Performing Arts: Many people think of the bluegrass sounds of Earl Scruggs when they think of the Tar Heel State. Folk, country, and gospel music all enjoy a strong following in the state. North Carolinians also actively support classical music. Raleigh hosts the North Carolina Symphony Orchestra. Greensboro, Charlotte, and Winston-Salem also have symphony orchestras. Raleigh, Greensboro, and Charlotte have opera companies.

The state is known for its historical pageants. *The Lost Colony*, the nation's longest-running outdoor drama, is staged every summer at Roanoke Island. *Unto These Hills*, about the Cherokee people, is performed at Cherokee. A Daniel Boone biography, *Horn of the West*, is performed at Boone.

Sports and Recreation: The Charlotte Hornets joined the National Basketball Association in 1988. The Durham Bulls are an avidly followed minor-league baseball team.

North Carolina schools provide some of the finest college basketball in the country. The University of North Carolina, North Carolina State, and Duke University usually field top-rated teams. All play in the competitive Atlantic Coast Conference. The University of North Carolina at Charlotte has recently become a basketball power.

College football is also popular in North Carolina. The state's schools have produced a number of football stars. Receiver Mike Quick attended North Carolina State. Linebacker Lawrence Taylor is a University of North Carolina alumnus.

North Carolinians may enjoy more than sixty state parks, forests, and historic sites. Beaches and resorts offer fishing, water sports, and sunbathing. Inland sounds provide excellent freshwater fishing and duck hunting. Golf and tennis are year-round sports. The western mountains provide many hiking trails, including a portion of the Appalachian Trail, which runs from Maine to Georgia.

Men in nineteenth-century military dress at Fort Macon State Park

Historic Sites and Landmarks:

Alamance Battlefield, near Burlington, was the site of the 1771 battle in which the Regulators were defeated by colonial militia.

Bentonville Battleground, in Johnston County, was the site of the largest and bloodiest Civil War battle fought in North Carolina.

Fort Macon State Park, near Morehead City, is a restored fort that was built in the 1840s to guard Beaufort's harbor.

Fort Raleigh National Historic Site, on Roanoke Island, was the site of the first attempted English settlement in what is now the United States.

Guilford Courthouse National Military Park, near Greensboro, preserves the site where British General Charles Cornwallis won a costly Revolutionary War battle.

Market House, in Fayetteville, once a slave market, stands at the site of the building where representatives from North Carolina ratified the U.S. Constitution in 1789.

Market Square in Fayetteville

Moores Creek National Battlefield, near Wilmington, was the site of the first Revolutionary War battle fought in North Carolina.

Oconaluftee Indian Village, in Cherokee, is a reproduction of an eighteenth-century Cherokee village.

Old Salem Historic District, in Winston-Salem, is a restored eighteenth-century Moravian village.

James K. Polk Memorial State Historic Site, in Pineville, features a replica of the eleventh President's log-cabin birthplace.

Carl Sandburg Home National Historic Site, near Flat Rock, was the home and farm of the beloved poet and author from 1945 to 1967.

Tryon Palace Restoration and Gardens, in New Bern, served as a colonial capitol and as the first state capitol.

USS North Carolina Battleship Memorial, in Wilmington, allows visitors to tour a battleship that took part in every major Pacific offensive of World War II.

The great World War II battleship USS *North Carolina* is now permanently docked at Wilmington and may be toured by the public.

Thomas Wolfe Memorial House, in Asheville, was the boyhood home of the noted writer. It has been designated a National Historic Landmark.

Wright Brothers National Memorial, near Kitty Hawk, marks the site of the first powered airplane flight.

Other Interesting Places to Visit:

Biltmore Estate, a lavish estate near Asheville, was the home of railroad magnate Cornelius Vanderbilt.

Blue Ridge Parkway is a scenic mountain parkway that runs through northwestern North Carolina from the Great Smoky Mountains National Park entrance near Cherokee to Shenandoah National Park in Virginia.

Cape Hatteras National Seashore stretches for 70 mi. (113 km) and covers 30,000 acres (12,141 hectares) on Bodie, Hatteras, and Ocracoke islands. A haven for wildlife, it features undisturbed beaches and dunes, as well as a self-guided tour of shipwrecks along the beach.

Cowee Valley Mines, near Franklin, offer "rockhounders" the chance to find rubies and other gemstones.

Grandfather Mountain, near Linville, has a mile-high (1.6-kilometer-high) swinging bridge that affords spectacular views.

Rockhounders may search for gemstones at a number of spots near Franklin in the Blue Ridge.

Great Smoky Mountains National Park, with its breathtaking mountain views and varied wildlife, is the nation's most frequently visited national park.

North Carolina Botanical Garden, in Chapel Hill, features hundreds of varieties of southeastern plants and trees.

North Carolina Zoological Park, near Asheboro, is one of the world's largest zoos. It has more than six hundred animals and ten thousand plants.

State Capitol, in Raleigh, is a classic Greek Revival structure that was built in 1840 and houses the governor's office.

State Legislative Building, in Raleigh, houses the North Carolina General Assembly.

World Golf Hall of Fame, in Pinehurst, displays photographs and memorabilia of many famous golfers.

IMPORTANT DATES

1524—Giovanni da Verrazano, an Italian explorer sailing for France, visits the Cape Fear area

1526—Lucas Vásquez de Ayllón, an explorer from Santo Domingo, founds a short-lived colony at Cape Fear

1540—Spanish explorer Hernando De Soto crosses the mountains of western North Carolina

When John White returned to Roanoke Island in 1590, he found no trace of the colonists he had left behind—only the puzzling word "Croatoan" carved into a tree.

1584 — Sir Walter Raleigh sends explorers to scout out a suitable site for a colony in the North Carolina region

1585 — At Roanoke Island, settlers sent by Raleigh establish the first English colony in what is now the United States

1586 — The colony at Roanoke Island fails and the colonists return to England

1587 — Sir Walter Raleigh sends a second group of settlers to Roanoke Island; Virginia Dare, the first child born of English parents in America, is born

1590 — English explorers return to Roanoke and find that the colony has disappeared; it henceforth becomes known as the Lost Colony

1629 — King Charles I of England grants a huge tract of North American land— including the land of present-day North Carolina and South Carolina—to Sir Robert Heath, who names it *Carolana* after the monarch (the spelling is later changed to *Carolina*)

1663 — King Charles II grants Carolina to eight lords proprietors

1664 — The North Carolina region's first permanent government is established in Albemarle County

1677 — Colonists rebel against the colonial governor in what becomes known as Culpeper's Rebellion

1705 — Bath becomes the first incorporated town in North Carolina

1710 — German, Swiss, and English settlers found New Bern

1711—The bloody, two-year-long Tuscarora War begins

1712—North Carolina and South Carolina become separate colonies

1729—North Carolina comes under the direct rule of the British monarch after the lords proprietors sell back their lands

1751—North Carolina's first newspaper, the *North Carolina Gazette*, is founded in New Bern

1760—Colonists led by Hugh Waddell defeat Cherokee Indians at Fort Dobbs

1771—In the Battle of Alamance Creek, rebellious frontiersmen known as the Regulators are defeated by colonial militia

1774—Women at Edenton sign a resolution protesting British injustice; North Carolina elects delegates to the First Continental Congress

1776—North Carolina delegates to the Continental Congress become the first to vote for independence from England; patriots defeat loyalists in the Battle of Moores Creek Bridge

1781—British General Charles Cornwallis defeats Americans at the Battle of Guilford Courthouse but suffers such heavy casualties that he soon surrenders at Yorktown in Virginia

1789—North Carolina ratifies the U.S. Constitution and joins the Union as the twelfth state

1792—Raleigh becomes the state capital

1795—The University of North Carolina, the nation's first state university, opens at Chapel Hill

1799—First significant deposit of gold in the United States is discovered at Reed Gold Mine

1835—A revised state constitution gives greater representation to the people of the western part of the state

1840—The state's first railroad, linking Wilmington with Weldon, is completed

1845—North Carolina native James K. Polk takes office as the eleventh U.S. president

1861—North Carolina secedes from the Union after the Confederate capture of Fort Sumter

1865 — After the bloody Battle of Bentonville, General Joseph E. Johnson surrenders to Union General William Tecumseh Sherman near Durham; North Carolina native Andrew Johnson takes office as seventeenth U.S. president

1868 — North Carolina is readmitted to the Union and adopts a new state constitution

1870 — Democrats regain control of the state legislature

1871 — Governor William Holden, a Republican, is impeached and removed from office

1877 — Reconstruction ends

1901 — Governor Charles Aycock begins a massive school-construction program

1903 — Wilbur and Orville Wright make the first successful powered airplane flight at Kitty Hawk

1915 — The newly formed State Highway Commission begins the most extensive road-building program in the state's history; as a result, North Carolina becomes known as the Good Roads State

1924 — James B. "Buck" Duke gives a $40 million endowment to Trinity College, which is then renamed Duke University

1936 — North Carolina Intracoastal Waterway is completed

1945 — Fontana Dam, the largest Tennessee Valley Authority dam, is completed; Kerr Dam begins operation

1958 — Construction begins on the Research Triangle Park in the Raleigh-Durham area

1959 — North Carolina becomes the first state in the South to pass a minimum-wage law

1960 — To protest segregation, four black students hold the nation's first "sit-in" at a Greensboro lunch counter

1965 — North Carolina School for the Arts, the nation's first state-supported school for the arts, opens in Winston-Salem

1971 — North Carolina's third state constitution goes into effect

1980 — J. P. Stevens textile company and Amalgamated Clothing and Textile Workers settle a seventeen-year labor dispute

1984 — Senator Jesse Helms defeats former governor Jim Hunt in the most expensive Senate election in American history

1988—A complicated corporate buy-out of Winston-Salem's R. J. Reynolds Company brings a great deal of money to small shareholders

IMPORTANT PEOPLE

Archie Randolph (A. R.) Ammons (1926-   ), born in Whiteville; poet; celebrated nature in such books as *Ommateum* and *Sphere: The Form of a Motion*; won National Book Award for poetry (1973)

Lucius Benjamin (Luke) Appling (1907-   ), born in High Point; baseball player; shortstop with Chicago White Sox (1930-50); won two American League batting championships; elected to Baseball Hall of Fame (1964)

Henry Atkinson (1782-1842), born in North Carolina; soldier, explorer; led expeditions to the Yellowstone River; commanded forces in the Blackhawk War; arranged many treaties with Indians

Charles Brantley Aycock (1859-1912), born near Goldsboro; statesman; governor (1901-05); his massive school-construction program earned him the nickname "Education Governor"

CHARLES AYCOCK

Thomas Hart Benton (1782-1858), born in Hillsborough; statesman; U.S. senator from Missouri (1821-51); opposed allowing slavery in the western territories; designed the plan that later became the Homestead Act

Daniel Boone (1734-1820), frontiersman; moved with his parents to North Carolina in 1750; opened up the wilderness beyond the eastern U.S. for American settlement; responsible for the Wilderness Road

Braxton Bragg (1817-1876), born in Warrenton; military leader; Confederate general; led Confederate troops to victory in Battle of Chickamauga; military advisor to Confederate President Jefferson Davis

BRAXTON BRAGG

David Brinkley (1920-   ), born in Wilmington; journalist; pioneered television newscasting with partner Chet Huntley; host of the television program "This Week with David Brinkley"

Charlotte Hawkins Brown (1883-1961), born in Henderson; educator; founded the American Missionary Association school at Sedalia (renamed Palmer Memorial Institute), one of the finest schools in the South founded for blacks

Robert Carlyle Byrd (1917-   ), born in North Wilkesboro; politician; U.S. senator from West Virginia (1959-   ); Senate majority leader (1977-81, 1987-89); Senate minority leader (1981-87)

DAVID BRINKLEY

JOHN COLTRANE

AUGUSTIN DALY

ELIZABETH DOLE

BILLY GRAHAM

Richard Caswell (1729-1789), soldier, statesman; led victorious forces at Moores Creek Bridge; helped write North Carolina's first state constitution; governor (1776-80, 1785-87)

Levi Coffin (1789-1877), born in New Garden; abolitionist leader; known as the "President of the Underground Railroad"

John William Coltrane (1926-1967), born in Hamlet; jazz musician; saxophonist known for his harmonic and melodic experiments and his technical virtuosity

Howard Cosell (1920-   ), born Howard Cohen in Winston-Salem; journalist; television sportscaster who gained fame for his "tell-it-like-it-is" style

John Augustin Daly (1838-1899), born in Plymouth; playwright, producer; established one of the most important theater companies on Broadway

Virginia Dare (1587-?), born on Roanoke Island; first English child born in what is now the United States; disappeared with the rest of the "Lost Colony" of Roanoke Island

William Richardson Davie (1756-1820), soldier, lawyer, statesman; helped draft U.S. Constitution; led successful movement for North Carolina statehood; governor (1798-99)

Elizabeth Hanford Dole (1936-   ), born in Salisbury; public official; first woman to serve as U.S. secretary of transportation (1983-87); U.S. secretary of labor (1989-   )

Benjamin Newton Duke (1855-1929) and **James Buchanan Duke** (1856-1925), born near Durham; businessmen, philanthropists; in 1890 established the American Tobacco Company; gave a huge endowment to Trinity College, which later became Duke University

Samuel James Ervin, Jr. (1896-1985), born in Morganton; politician; U.S. senator (1954-75); leading authority on the U.S. Constitution; presided over the 1973 Senate Watergate hearings

Donna Fargo (1949-   ), born in Mt. Airy; singer; recorded such country-music hits as "Funny Face" and "I'm the Happiest Girl in the Whole U.S.A."

Roberta Flack (1940-   ), born in Black Mountain; singer; won a Grammy Award for "The First Time Ever I Saw Your Face"

Richard Jordan Gatling (1818-1903), born in North Carolina; inventor; improved farm machinery; invented the Gatling gun, a quick-firing machine gun

William Franklin (Billy) Graham (1918-   ), born in Charlotte; evangelist; conducts religious crusades throughout the world; befriended presidents Eisenhower, Johnson, and Nixon; wrote *Peace with God* and *How to Be Born Again*

Frank Porter Graham (1886-1972), born in Fayetteville; educator; created plan to consolidate the state university system; president of University of North Carolina (1930-49)

Paul Eliot Green (1894-1981), born in Lillington; playwright; won 1927 Pulitzer Prize in drama for *In Abraham's Bosom*; wrote historical "symphonic dramas" such as *The Lost Colony* and *Trumpet in the Land,* as well as plays and novels about life in the South; known as the "Father of American Outdoor Drama"

PAUL GREEN

Andy Griffith (1926-   ), born in Mt. Airy; actor; best known for his role as Sheriff Andy Taylor on the television program "The Andy Griffith Show"

Jesse Alexander Helms (1921-   ), born in Monroe; politician; U.S. senator (1973-   ) known for his conservative views

William Hooper (1742-1790), statesman; settled in Wilmington; member of Continental Congress (1774-77) and all five North Carolina provincial congresses; signer of Declaration of Independence

James B. Hunt, Jr. (1937-   ), born in Greensboro; politician; governor (1977-85); as governor, pushed for school competency tests, attracted outside investment, and supported civil rights

ANDY GRIFFITH

Jim "Catfish" Hunter (1946-   ), born in Hertford; baseball player; won more than 200 games with the Athletics and Yankees; led his teams to five world championships; elected to Baseball Hall of Fame (1987)

James Iredell (1751-1799), statesman, jurist; attorney general of North Carolina (1779-81); led the effort to have North Carolina ratify the U.S. Constitution; one of the original justices of the U.S. Supreme Court (1790-99)

Andrew Johnson (1808-1875), born in Raleigh; seventeenth president of the U.S. (1865-69); U.S. representative from Tennessee (1843-53); governor of Tennessee (1853-57); U.S. senator from Tennessee (1857-62); vice-president of the U.S. (1865); became president after Abraham Lincoln was assassinated; although he was impeached as a result of his disagreements with Congress over Reconstruction policies, he was acquitted and was not removed from office

JESSE HELMS

Michael Jordan (1963-   ), basketball player; grew up in Wilmington; led University of North Carolina to the NCAA championship in 1982; starred for U.S. Olympic basketball team in 1984; one of the NBA's highest-scoring players; considered basketball's most exciting slam-dunk star

William Rufus de Vane King (1786-1853), born in Sampson County; politician; U.S. senator from Alabama (1819-44, 1848-53); U.S. minister to France (1844-46); vice-president of the U.S. (1853); died shortly after assuming office

MICHAEL JORDAN

KAY KYSER

DOLLEY MADISON

FLOYD McKISSICK

EDWARD R. MURROW

Charles Kuralt (1934-   ), born in Wilmington; television journalist; best known for his "On the Road" reports in which he journeys around America

Kay Kyser (1905-1985), born in Rocky Mount; musician; entertained radio audiences with his "Kollege of Musical Knowledge"

Herman Warden Lay (1909-1982), born in Charlotte; businessman; founder and president of the Frito Lay food company (1939-65); Chairman of Pepsico Inc. (1965-71)

Ray "Sugar Ray" Leonard (1956-   ), born in Wilmington; boxer; won 1976 Olympic gold medal for U.S.; held world welterweight titles (1979, 1980, 1981-82); held WBC middleweight title (1987)

Dolley Payne Madison (1786-1849), born in Guilford County; Washington socialite; wife of President James Madison; served as a leading advisor to her husband and as social leader of Washington, D.C.; rescued a portrait of George Washington when British burned the White House during War of 1812

Floyd Bixler McKissick (1922-   ), born in Asheville; lawyer, civil-rights activist; national chairman of Congress of Racial Equality (CORE) (1963-66); national director of CORE (1966-68)

Thelonious Sphere Monk (1920-1981), pianist and composer; one of the creators of the "bop" style of jazz; best-known songs include "Round Midnight" and "Blue Monk"

Edward R. Murrow (1908-1965), born in Greensboro; journalist; during World War II, made stirring broadcasts from England to American radio audiences; produced and hosted "Person to Person" and "See It Now" television programs; director of the U.S. Information Agency (1961-64)

Kenneth Noland (1924-   ), born in Asheville; one of America's foremost abstract artists

Walter Hines Page (1855-1918), born in Cary; journalist, diplomat; wrote syndicated articles on social and economic problems in the South; ambassador to Great Britain (1913-18); advocated U.S. entry into World War I

John Penn (1740-1788), statesman; member of North Carolina provincial legislature and Continental Congress; signer of Declaration of Independence

Gaylord Perry (1938-   ), born in Williamston; baseball player; only pitcher to win the Cy Young Award in both the American League (1972) and National League (1978); during his 22-year career, amassed a total of 314 victories

James Knox Polk (1795-1849), born in Mecklenburg County; eleventh president of the U.S. (1845-49); expanded U.S. by settling Oregon boundary with Great Britain and by annexing Mexican territory (California and most of the Southwest) after successfully conducting Mexican War

Leonidas Polk (1806-1864), born in Raleigh; clergyman, soldier; cousin of James K. Polk; served as Episcopal bishop of Louisiana; Confederate general who commanded forces in the battles of Shiloh, Murfreesboro, and Chickamauga

Leonidas L. Polk (1837-1892), farmer, editor; helped form the Farmers' Alliance; started the newspaper the *Progressive Farmer*

JAMES POLK

William Sydney Porter (1862-1910), wrote under the pen name O. Henry; born in Greensboro; writer; best known for the unexpected endings of his short stories; wrote ''The Gift of the Magi'' and ''The Ransom of Red Chief''

Sir Walter Raleigh (1522?-1618), English courtier; though he never came to North Carolina himself, he twice sent English settlers to establish a permanent colony on Roanoke Island

Hiram Rhoades Revels (1822-1901), born in Fayetteville; clergyman, educator, politician; helped establish black churches and schools in the Midwest and South; first black elected to U.S. Senate (representing Mississippi) (1870-71)

WALTER RALEIGH

Joseph Rhine (1895-1980), psychologist; founder and director of Institute of Parapsychology at Duke University (1964-68)

Terry Sanford (1917-   ), politician, educator; governor (1961-65); as governor, instituted innovative educational programs; president of Duke University (1969-85); U.S. senator (1986-   )

Earl Scruggs (1924-   ), born in Cleveland County; musician; revolutionized bluegrass music with his five-string banjo playing

Enos Slaughter (1916-   ), born in Roxboro; baseball player; thrilled St. Louis Cardinals and New York Yankees fans with his aggressive playing style; led his teams to four world championships; elected to Baseball Hall of Fame (1985)

HIRAM REVELS

Zebulon Baird Vance (1830-1894), born in Buncombe County; soldier, politician; U.S. representative (1858-61); served in the Confederate army (1861-62); governor (1862-66, 1876-78); as governor during the Civil War, led successful efforts to arm the state's soldiers and supply residents with food and clothing; U.S. senator (1879-94)

Cornelius Vanderbilt (1794-1877), financier; amassed a huge fortune through his dealings in the railroad business; constructed elaborate Biltmore Estate in Asheville

Thomas Clayton Wolfe (1900-1938), born in Asheville; writer; known for such autobiographical novels as *Look Homeward, Angel* and *You Can't Go Home Again*

ZEBULON VANCE

GOVERNORS

Richard Caswell	1776-1780	W. W. Holden	1865
Abner Nash	1780-1781	Jonathan Worth	1865-1868
Thomas Burke	1781-1782	W. W. Holden	1868-1871
Alexander Martin	1782-1784	T. R. Caldwell	1871-1874
Richard Caswell	1784-1787	C. H. Brogden	1874-1877
Samuel Johnston	1787-1789	Zebulon Vance	1877-1879
Alexander Martin	1789-1792	T. J. Jarvis	1879-1885
R. D. Spaight, Sr.	1792-1795	A. M. Scales	1885-1889
Samuel Ashe	1795-1798	D. G. Fowle	1889-1891
W. R. Davie	1798-1799	Thomas M. Holt	1891-1893
Benjamin Williams	1799-1802	Elias Carr	1893-1897
James Turner	1802-1805	D. L. Russell	1897-1901
Nathaniel Alexander	1805-1807	Charles B. Aycock	1901-1905
Benjamin Williams	1807-1808	R. B. Glenn	1905-1909
David Stone	1808-1810	W. W. Kitchin	1909-1913
Benjamin Smith	1810-1811	Locke Craig	1913-1917
William Hawkins	1811-1814	Thomas W. Bickett	1917-1921
William Miller	1814-1817	Cameron Morrison	1921-1925
John Branch	1817-1820	Angus Wilton McLean	1925-1929
Jesse Franklin	1820-1821	O. Max Gardner	1929-1933
Gabriel Holmes	1821-1824	J. C. B. Ehringhaus	1933-1937
H. G. Burton	1824-1827	Clyde R. Hoey	1937-1941
James Iredell, Jr.	1827-1828	J. Melville Broughton	1941-1945
John Owen	1828-1830	R. Gregg Cherry	1945-1949
Montfort Stokes	1830-1832	W. Kerr Scott	1949-1953
D. L. Swain	1832-1835	William B. Umstead	1953-1954
R. D. Spaight, Jr.	1835-1836	Luther H. Hodges	1954-1961
E. B. Dudley	1836-1841	Terry Sanford	1961-1965
J. M. Morehead	1841-1845	Daniel K. Moore	1965-1969
W. A. Graham	1845-1849	Robert W. Scott	1969-1973
Charles Manly	1849-1851	James E. Holshouser, Jr.	1973-1977
D. S. Reid	1851-1854	James B. Hunt, Jr.	1977-1985
Warren Winslow	1854-1855	James G. Martin	1985-
Thomas Bragg	1855-1859		
John W. Ellis	1859-1861		
Henry T. Clark	1861-1862		
Zebulon Vance	1862-1865		

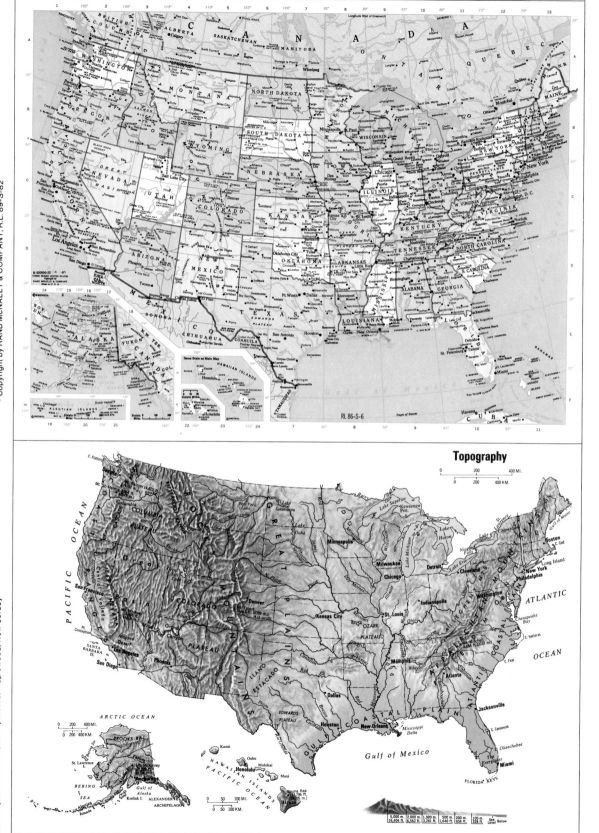

Topography

MAP KEY

Place	Grid
Aberdeen	B3
Ahoskie	A6
Albemarle	B2
Albemarle Sound (sound)	A6
Alexander Mills	B2
Alligator River (river)	B6
Andrews	f9
Angier	B4
Ansonville	B2
Apex	B4
Archdale	B3
Arlington	A2
Asheboro	B3
Asheville	f10
Atlantic	C6
Aulander	A5
Ayden	B5
Badin	B2
Badin Lake (lake)	B2
Balfour	f10
Banner Elk	f10
Barker Heights	f10
Bayboro	B6
Beaufort	C6
Belhaven	B6
Belmont	B1
Benjamin Everett Jordan Lake (lake)	B3
Benson	B4
Bessemer City	B1
Bethel	B5
Beulaville	C5
Biltmore Forest	f10
Biscoe	B3
Black Mountain	f10
Black River (river)	C4
Bladenboro	C4
Blowing Rock	A1
Blue Ridge Mountains	B1
Boger City	B1
Boiling Springs	B1
Bonnie Doone	B4
Boone	A1
Boonville	A2
Brevard	f10
Bryson City	f9
Buies Creek	B4
Burgaw	C5
Burlington	A3
Burnsville	f10
Butner	A4
Candor	B3
Canton	f10
Cape Fear (cape)	D5
Cape Fear River (river)	C4
Cape Hatteras	B7
Cape Lookout	C6
Carolina Beach	D5
Carrboro	B3
Carthage	B4
Cary	B4

Place	Grid
Castle Hayne	C5
Catawba River (river)	B2
Chadbourn	C4
Chapel Hill	B3
Cherryville	B1
China Grove	B2
Chowan River (river)	A6
Claremont	B1
Clayton	B4
Clemmons	A2
Clinton	C4
Clyde	f10
Coastal Plain	C4
Coats	B4
Columbia	B6
Columbus	f10
Concord	B2
Conover	B2
Cooleemee	B2
Cordova	B3
Cornelius	B1
Cramerton	B1
Creedmoor	A4
Cricket	A1
Cross Mill	B1
Crouse	B1
Cullowhee	f9
Cumberland	C4
Dallas	B1
Dan River (river)	A2
Davidson	B1
Deep River (river)	B3
Denton	B2
Dobson	A2
Drexel	B1
Dunn	B4
Durham	B4
East Flat Rock	f10
East Rockingham	B3
East Spencer	B2
Eden	A3
Edenton	A6
Elizabeth City	A6
Elizabethtown	C4
Elkin	A2
Ellerbe	B3
Elm City	B5
Elon College	A3
Enfield	A5
Enka	f10
Erwin	B4
Fair Bluff	C4
Fair Grove	B1
Fairmont	C4
Farmville	B5
Fayetteville	C4
Fishing Creek (creek)	A5
Flat River (river)	A4
Flat Rock	f10
Fletcher	f10
Fontana Lake (reservoir)	B4

Place	Grid
Forest City	B1
Four Oaks	B4
Franklin	f9
Franklinton	A4
Fremont	B5
French Broad River (river)	B4
Fuquay-Varina	B4
Garland	C4
Garner	B4
Garysburg	A5
Gaston	A5
Gastonia	B1
Gibsonville	A3
Glen Raven	A3
Goldsboro	B5
Graham	A3
Grandfather Mountain (mountain)	A1
Granite Falls	B1
Granite Quarry	B2
Great Dismal Swamp (swamp)	A6
Great Island (island)	B6
Great Pee Dee River (river)	B3
Great Smoky Mountains	f9
Green Swamp (swamp)	C4
Greensboro	A3
Greenville	B5
Grifton	B5
Gull Island (island)	B6
Hamlet	B3
Harkers Island	C6
Havelock	C6
Haw River	A3
Haw River (river)	B3
Hays	A1
Hazelwood	f10
Henderson	A4
Hendersonville	f10
Henrietta	B1
Hertford	A6
Hickory	B1
Hiddenite	B2
High Point	B2
High Rock Lake (lake)	B2
Hillsborough	A3
Hog Island (island)	B6
Hope Mills	C4
Hudson	B1
Hyco Lake (lake)	A3
Indian Trail	B2
Jacksonville	C5
James, Lake (lake)	B1
Jamestown	B3
Jamesville	B6
Jefferson	A1
John H. Kerr Reservoir (reservoir)	A4
Jonesville	A2
Kannapolis	B2
Kenansville	C4
Kenly	B4
Kernersville	A2
King	A2
Kings Mountain	B1
Kinston	B5
Knightdale	B4
La Grange	B5
Lafayette	C4
Lake Waccamaw	C4
Landis	B2
Laurel Hill	B3
Laurinburg	C3
Lenoir	B1
Lexington	B2
Liberty	B3
Lillington	B4
Lincolnton	B1
Little River (river)	D4
Little River Inlet (inlet)	D5
Littleton	A5
Long View	B1
Louisburg	A4
Lowell	B1
Lucama	B5
Lumber River (river)	C3
Lumberton	C3
Lure, Lake (lake)	f10
Madison	A2
Maiden	B1
Manteo	B6
Marion	f10
Marshall	f10
Marshville	B2
Matthews	B2
Mattamuskeet, Lake (lake)	B6
Maxton	C3

Place	Grid
Mayodan	A3
Maysville	C5
Mebane	A3
Middlesex	B4
Midland	B2
Mint Hill	B2
Misenheimer	B2
Mitchell, Mount (mountain)	f10
Mocksville	B2
Monroe	B2
Montreat	f10
Mooresville	B1
Morehead City	C6
Morganton	B1
Morven	B2
Mount Airy	A2
Mount Gilead	B3
Mount Holly	B1
Mount Olive	B4
Mount Pleasant	B2
Moyock	A6
Mulberry	A1
Murfreesboro	A5
Murphy	f8
Nags Head	B7
Nashville	B5
Neuse River (river)	B5
New Bern	B6
New Lake (lake)	B6
New River (river)	C5
Newland	A1
Newport	C6
Newton	B1
Norlina	A4
Norman, Lake (lake)	B1
North Belmont	B1
North East Cape Fear River (river)	C4
North Wilkesboro	A1
Norwood	B2
Oak Ridge	A3
Ocracoke Island (island)	B7
Old Fort	B1
Oteen	f10
Oxford	A4
Pamlico River (river)	B6
Parkwood	B4
Paw Creek	B1
Pembroke	C3
Phelps Lake (lake)	B6
Piedmont Plateau	B2
Pilot Mountain	A2
Pine Level	B4
Pinebluff	B3
Pinehurst	B3
Pinetops	B5
Pineville	B1
Pisgah Forest	f10
Pittsboro	B3
Pleasant Garden	A3
Plymouth	B6
Polkton	B2
Princeton	B4
Princeville	B5
Pungo Lake (lake)	B6
Raeford	C3
Raleigh	B4
Raleigh Bay (bay)	C6
Ramseur	B3
Randleman	B3
Red Springs	C3
Reidsville	A3
Rhodhiss	B1
Rich Square	A5
Richlands	C5
Roanoke Island (island)	B7
Roanoke Rapids	A5
Roanoke Rapids Lake (lake)	A5
Roanoke River (river)	B3
Robbinsville	f9
Robersonville	B5
Rockingham	B3
Rockwell	B2
Rockwell Park	B2
Rocky Mount	B5
Rocky River (river)	B2
Roper	B6
Rose Hill	C4
Roseboro	C4
Rowland	C3
Roxboro	A4
Royal Pines	f10
Rural Hall	A2
Rutherfordton	B1
Salemburg	C4
Salisbury	B2
Sanford	B4
Scotland Neck	A5

Place	Grid
Scott Reservoir (reservoir)	A1
Selma	B4
Sharpsburg	B5
Shelby	B1
Siler City	B3
Skyland	f10
Smithfield	B4
Snow Hill	B5
South Gastonia	B1
South Hill	A6
South Mills	C4
South River (river)	C3
Southern Pines	B3
Southmont	B2
Southport	D4
Sparta	A1
Spencer	B2
Spindale	B1
Spring Hope	B4
Spring Lake	B3
Spruce Pine	f10
St. Pauls	C4
Stanley	B1
Stanleyville	A2
Stantonsburg	B5
Star	B3
State Road	A2
Statesville	B2
Stedman	B4
Stokesdale	A3
Stoneville	A3
Stony Point	B1
Summerfield	A3
Swannanoa	f10
Swansboro	C5
Swepsonville	A3
Swift Creek (creek)	B5
Sylva	f9
Tabor City	C4
Tar River (river)	B4
Tarboro	B5
Taylorsville	B1
Thomasville	B2
Tillery, Lake (lake)	B2
Toast	A2
Trent River (river)	B5
Troutman	B2
Troy	B3
Tryon	f10
Tuxedo	f10
Unaka Mountains	e10
Unicoi Mountains	f8
Uwharrie River (river)	B3
Valdese	B1
Vanceboro	B5
Vander	B4
Vass	B3
Waccamaw, Lake (lake)	C4
Waccamaw River (river)	C4
Wadesboro	B3
Wake Forest	B4
Walkertown	A2
Wallace	C4
Walnut Cove	A2
Wanchese	B7
Warrenton	A4
Warsaw	C4
Washington	B5
Waxhaw	B2
Waynesville	f10
Weaverville	f10
Weldon	A5
Wendell	B4
West Concord	B2
West End	B3
West Jefferson	A1
West Marion	f10
Whitakers	A5
Whiteville	C4
Wilkesboro	A1
Williamston	B5
Wilmington	C5
Wilson	B5
Windsor	A6
Wingate	B2
Winston-Salem	A2
Winterville	B5
Winton	A5
Woodland	A5
Wrightsville Beach	C5
Wylie, Lake (reservoir)	B1
Yadkin River (river)	B2
Yadkin Valley	A1
Yadkinville	A2
Yanceyville	A3
Zebulon	B4

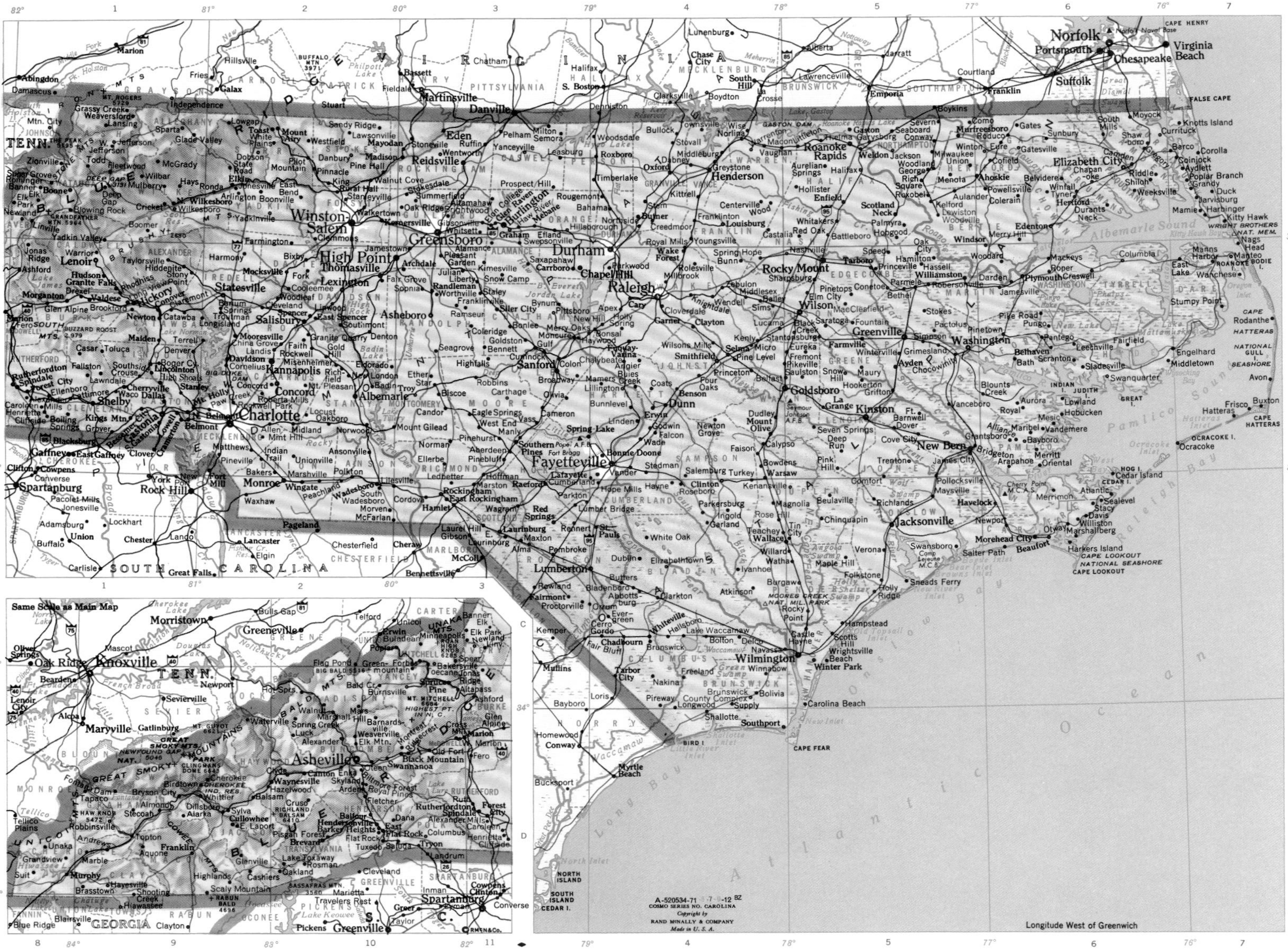
Norfolk
Virginia Beach
Chesapeake
Portsmouth
Suffolk
Winston Salem
Greensboro
High Point
Durham
Raleigh
Charlotte
Fayetteville
Wilmington
Rocky Mount
Wilson
Greenville
Goldsboro
Kinston
New Bern
Jacksonville
Asheville
Knoxville
Spartanburg
Greenville
Albemarle Sound
Pamlico Sound
Atlantic Ocean
CAPE HATTERAS
CAPE LOOKOUT
CAPE FEAR
Same Scale as Main Map
TENN.
GEORGIA
SOUTH CAROLINA
Longitude West of Greenwich
A-520534-71
COMMO SERIES NO. CAROLINA
Copyright by
RAND McNALLY & COMPANY
Made in U. S. A.

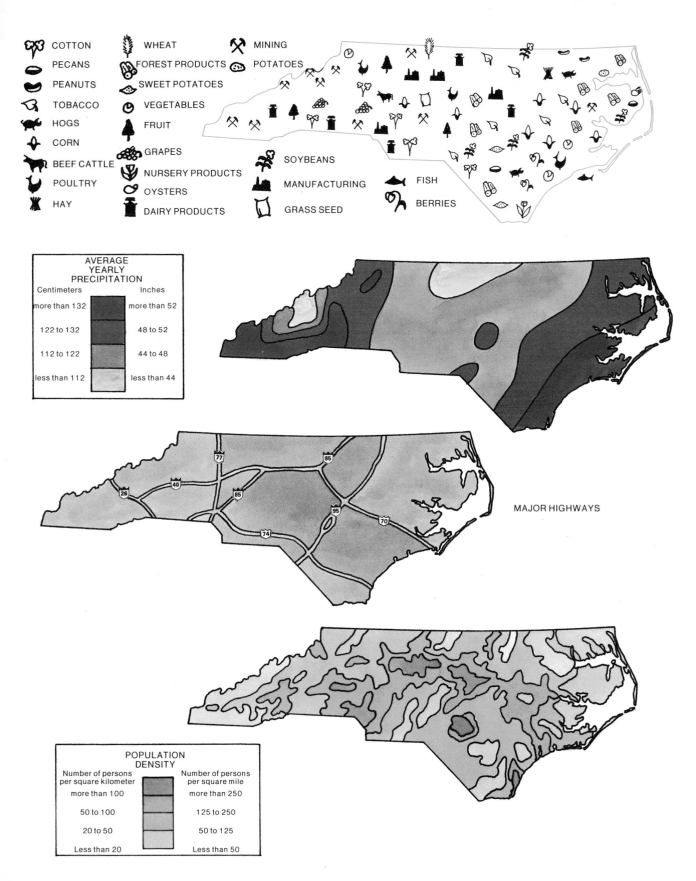

COTTON
PECANS
PEANUTS
TOBACCO
HOGS
CORN
BEEF CATTLE
POULTRY
HAY

WHEAT
FOREST PRODUCTS
SWEET POTATOES
VEGETABLES
FRUIT
GRAPES
NURSERY PRODUCTS
OYSTERS
DAIRY PRODUCTS

MINING
POTATOES

SOYBEANS
MANUFACTURING
GRASS SEED

FISH
BERRIES

AVERAGE
YEARLY
PRECIPITATION

Centimeters		Inches
more than 132		more than 52
122 to 132		48 to 52
112 to 122		44 to 48
less than 112		less than 44

MAJOR HIGHWAYS

POPULATION
DENSITY

Number of persons per square kilometer		Number of persons per square mile
more than 100		more than 250
50 to 100		125 to 250
20 to 50		50 to 125
Less than 20		Less than 50

TOPOGRAPHY

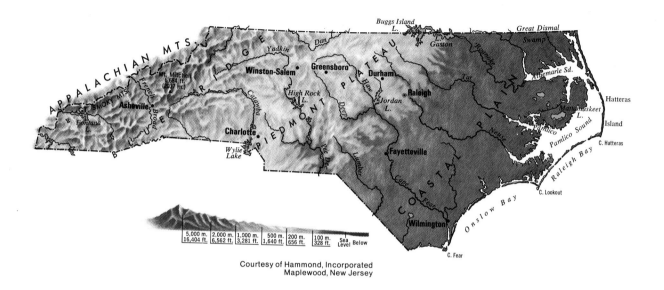

Courtesy of Hammond, Incorporated
Maplewood, New Jersey

COUNTIES

Orton Plantation in Brunswick County

INDEX

Page numbers that appear in boldface type indicate illustrations

Ackland Art Museum, 81, 98
agriculture, 11, 17, 26, 35-36, 45, 46, 58, 72-73, **73**, 117
Airlie Gardens, 94
Alamance Battlefield, 99, 120
Alamance Creek, Battle of, 37, 125
Albemarle, 101, 114
Albemarle Museum, 95
Albemarle Sound, 31
Alexander, Hezekiah, home of, 101
Alligator Lake, 112
Amadas, Philip, 29
American Tobacco Company, 56-57
Ammons, Archie Randolph, 127
animals, 15, **15**, 16, 114

Appalachian Mountains, 11
Appalachian Trail, 105, 119
Appling, Luke, 127
Arrington, Katherine P., 81
art, **24-25**, **78-79**, 80-82, **81**, 88
Asheboro, 123
Asheville, 21, 43, 88, 110, 113, 114, 116, 122
Atkinson, Henry, 127
Atlantic Coastal Plain, 10-11, 13, 14, 15, 16-17, 22, 36, 73, 95-97, 112, 113, 114
Atlantic Intracoastal Waterway, 117, 126
Atlantic Ocean, 10, 13, 22
auto racing, 88, 101
Aycock, Charles, 60, 126, 127, **127**

Ayllón, Lucas Vásquez, 123
Bald Head Lighthouse, 94
Banner Elk, 105
Barbell, John, 80
Barlowe, Arthur, 29
Baskerville, Charles, Jr., 81
Bath, 32, 33, 95, 118, 124
Batts, Nathaniel, 31
beaches, 11-12
Bearden, Romare, 82
  painting by, **78-79**
Beatty, Jim, 87
Beaufort, 12, 34, 95, 118
Belmont, 103, 116
Benson, 89
Benton, Thomas Hart, 127
Bentonville, 50
  Battle of, 120, 126

138

Biltmore Estate, 106, **106**, 122
birds, **14**, 16, 114, **114**
  state, **108**, 109
Blackbeard, 33-34
Black Mountain, 88, 113
blacks, 21, **52**, 53, 59-60
Blowing Rock, 80, 105
Blue Ridge Folk Art Center, **89**
Blue Ridge Mountains, 11, 22,
  27, 28, 34, 36, 43, 92, 107, 112,
  113, **123**
Blue Ridge Parkway **90-91**, **103**,
  104, **107**, 122
Bodie Island Lighthouse, **2-3**
Boggs Lake, 13-14
Bogue Sound, **118**
Boiling Springs, 116
Bonney, Anne, 33, **33**
Boone, 104, 105, 119
Boone, Daniel, 34, 127
Boonesboro, 34
borders, 10, 111
Bragg, Braxton, 127, **127**
Bridal Veil Falls, 106
Brinkley, David, 84, 127, **127**
Broad River, 112
Brown, Charlotte Hawkins, 127
Brunswick, 34, 97
Buies Creek, 116
Burgwin-Wright House, 96
Burlington, 99, 120
Burnsville, 105
business, 61, 117
Byrd, Robert Carlyle, 127
Calabash, 94-95
Campbelltown, 35
Camp Lejeune, 63, 77
Cannon, J. W., 57
Cannon Textile Company, 102
cape, 12
Cape Fear, 12, 28, 94, 113
Cape Fear River, 13, 112
Cape Hatteras, **4**, 12, **12**, 29, **49**,
  50, **94**, 113
Cape Hatteras Lighthouse, **12**,
  94
Cape Hatteras National
  Seashore, 92, 111, 122
Cape Lookout, 12, 113

Cape Lookout National
  Seashore, 16, 111, **113**
Carolana, 31
Carowinds, 102
carpetbaggers, 51
Caswell, Richard, 38, 128
Catawba Indians, 27
Catawba River, 112
Ceasar, Shirley, 85
Chadbourn, 88
Chapel Hill, 42, 72, 77, 81-82,
  87, 98-99, 116, 118, 123
Charity Sisters, 85-86
Charles I, 31, 124
Charles II, 32, 124
Charlotte, 10, 17, 21, 66, 72, 74,
  101-103, 110, 114, 116, 117,
  118, 119
Charlotte Motor Speedway, 88,
  102
Charlotte Nature Museum, 102,
  118
Cheraw Indians, 27
Cherokee, 87, 106, 119, 121
Cherokee Indian Reservation, 21
Cherokee Indians, 21-22, 43-44,
  105-106, 125
Cherry Point Marine Air
  Station, 63
Chimney Rock, 106
Chowan River, 13, 31
Civilian Conservation Corps, 62
civil rights movement, **64**, 65,
  126
Civil War, 47, 48, **49**, 50-51, **50**,
  125-126
Clayton, 88
climate, 16-17, 26, 114, **136**
Clinton, 89
coast, 11-12, **14**, 17, 113
Coffin, Levi, 128
Coleman, Warren, 59, **59**
Coleman Manufacturing
  Company, 59
colleges and universities, 42, 46,
  62, 64, 71, 116, **116**
colors, state, 109
Coltrane, John, 85, 128, **128**
communications, 61, 77, 117

Concord, 116
Congress of Racial Equality, 65
Connestee Falls, 106
constitution, 39, 44-45, 46, 48,
  125, 126
Continental Congress, 37, 125
Cooper, Anna, 59
Corees, 27
Cornwallis, Charles, 7, 38, 120,
  125
Cosell, Howard, 128
courts, 70, 115
Cowee Valley Mines, 122
Croatan Indians, 27, 30-31
Croatan National Forest, 95
Culpeper's Rebellion, 32, 124
Daingerfield, Elliot, 80
Daly, John Augustin, 128, **128**
Dare, Eleanor, 30
Dare, Virginia, **24-25**, 30, 124,
  128
Dare Days, 88
Davidson, 71, 116
Davie, William Richardson, 42,
  128
Davis, Jefferson, 48
Deep Gap, 85
Denim Fun Days, 88
De Soto, Hernando, 28, 123
Discovery Place, 102
Dismal Swamp, 11, **114**
Dismal Swamp Canal **40-41**
Dole, Elizabeth Hanford, 128,
  128
Duke, Benjamin **57**, 128
Duke, James, 56, **57**, 62, 126, 128
Duke, Washington, 56
Duke University, 46, 62, 71, **71**,
  77, 87, 99, 116, 118, 119
Durant, George, 31
Durham, 20, 21, 56, 64, 71, 76,
  77, 99, 110, 116
East, John, 67
economy, 42, 46, 53, 61-63, 65,
  66, 70, 72-73, 117
Edenton, 32, 95, 125
education, 45-46, **45**, 53, 60, 61,
  64, 65-66, 70-72, 116
Elon College, 116

Elizabeth City, 95
Elizabethtown, 97
Ervin, Samuel James, Jr., 20, 128
Erwin, 88
ethnic peoples, 21, 34-35
European settlement, 28-34
Fall Line, 13, 113
Fargo, Donna, 128
Farmers' Alliance, 58
Fayetteville, 21, 35, 39, 63, 95,
  110, 116, 120, **121**
Ferry, Danny, 87
festivals, 88-89, **89**
fish, 15-16, 114
fishing, 74
Flack, Roberta, 85, 128
flag, state, **108**, 109
Flat Rock Playhouse, 106
flowers, **14**, 15, **15**, **103**
  state, **108**, 109
Fontana Dam, 126
Fontana Lake, 112
Fort Bragg, 63, 77
Fort Dobbs, 125
Fort Fisher State Historic Site, 94
Fort Macon State Park, 120,
  120
Fort Ocracoke, **49**
Fort Raleigh, 93, 120
Fort Sumter, 48, 125
Franklin, 122, **123**
French and Indian War, 37
French Broad River, 112
Gaston, William, 110
Gaston Blues, **49**
Gastonia, 103, 110
Gatling, Richard, 128
gemstone, state, 109
General Assembly, 69-70, 115,
  115
geography, 10, 111-114
George III, 34, 35
gold mining, 46, 47, **46**
Goldsboro, 63
government, 52, 69-70, 115
governors, 69, 115, 132
Graham, Frank Porter, 129
Graham, William (Billy), 23, 84,
  128, **128**

Grandfather Mountain, 89, 104,
  104, 122
Great Depression, 62, **62**
Great Smoky Mountains, **8-9**, 11,
  113
Great Smoky Mountains
  National Park, 11, 92, 105,
  105, 111, 122, 123
Green, John Ruffin, 56
Green, Paul Eliot, 86, 129, **129**
Greenfield Gardens, **97**
Greensboro, 20, 21, 65, 66, 72,
  74, 76, 81, 82, 99, 110, 111,
  116, 117, 118, 119, 120
Griffith, Andy, 86, 129, **129**
Guilford Courthouse, Battle of,
  38, 125
Guilford Courthouse National
  Military Park, 111, 120
Halifax, 39
Hamlet, 85
Hammocks Beach State Park, 94
Hanging Rock State Park, 100
Hatteras Indians, 27
Havelock, 63
Heath, Sir Robert, 31, 124
Helms, Jesse, 67, 84, 126, 129,
  129
Helper, Hinton Rowan, 83
Hickory, 116, 118
Highland Games and Scottish
  Clan Gathering, 88-89
Highlands, 106
High Point, 21, 100, 110, 116
High Point College, 116
High Rock Lake, 13
Hillsborough, 37, 39, 99
Hillsborough Convention, 38-39
historic sites and landmarks,
  120-122
history, 26-67, 123-127
Hodges, Luther, 64
Holden, William, 52, 126
Holshouser, James E., Jr., 66-67
Hooper, William, 129
Horton, George Moses, 83
Hunt, James B., Jr., 126, 129
Hunter, Kermit, 86
Indians, 21-22, 26-28

industry, 14, 36, **36**, 46-47, 53,
  54-55, 56-57, 62, 67, 69, 100,
  117
insect, state, 109
Iredell, James, 129
Jackson, Andrew, 43, 101
Jacksonville, 63
Janzen, Christen, 10
"Jim Crow" laws, 60, 65
Jockey's Ridge State Park, 93
Johnson, Andrew, 43, 126, 129
Johnson, Joseph E., 126
Johnson, Seymour, Air Force
  Base, 63, 77
Jones, Bobby, 87
Jones, H. G., 46
Jordan, Michael, 87, 129, **129**
Kannapolis, 57, 102
Kenley, 95
Kentucky, 34
Kerr Dam, 126
Kerr Lake, 13-14, 86, 112
Key, Alexander, 84
Keyauwees, 27
Kill Devil Hills, 92-93
King, William Rufus de Vane,
  129
Kingston, 76
Kitty Hawk, 61, **61**, 92, 122, 126
Ku Klux Klan, 51-52
Kuralt, Charles, 84, 130
Kyser, Kay, 130, **130**
Lake Hickory, 13
Lake Lure, 106
Lake Mattamuskeet, 14, 112
Lake Norman, 13, 102, **112**
lakes, 13-14, 112
Lake Waccamaw State Park, 97
Lane, Lunsford, 47
Lane, Ralph, 29-30
Latta Place, 101
Laurinburg, 116
Lawson, John, 32, 82
Lay, Herman Warden, 130
legislative branch, 69-70
Leonard, Ray "Sugar Ray," 87,
  130
Lexington, 76
libraries, 118

Canned vegetables from a North Carolina farm

Lincoln, Abraham, 48
Linville, 104, 122
Linville Caverns, 104
Linville Falls, 104
literature, 82-84
Little Roanoke River, 112
Little Tennessee River, 112
Lizard Lick, 89
Lost Colony, 30-31, 86, 93, 119, 124, **124**
Loudermilk, John D., 85
loyalists, 38
Lumberton, 97
Madison, Dolley, 130, **130**
mammal, state, **108**, 109
Manteo, 88
manufacturing, 74-76, **75**, **76**, 117
maps of North Carolina,
   counties, **137**
   major highways, **136**
   political, **135**
   population, **136**
   precipitation, **136**
   principal products, **136**
   topography, **137**
maps of United States,
   political, **133**
   topography, **133**
Market House, 120
Market Square, **121**
Mattison, Donald, 81

McAdenville, 103
McKissick, Floyd, 65, 130, **130**
Mecklenburg County
   Courthouse, **102**
Milsap, Ronnie, 85
minerals, 74
Mint Museum of Art, 102, 118
Monk, Thelonious, 130
Monroe, 101
Moores Creek Bridge, Battle of, 125
Moores Creek National
   Battlefield, 38, 97, 111, 121
Morehead City, 12, 95, 117, **118**, 120
Morehead Planetarium, 99, 118
Morrison, Cameron, 61
Morrow Mountain, 26, 101
motto, state, 7, 109
Mountain Region, 10, 11, 13, 17, 74, 103-107, 113, 114
Mount Mitchell, 111, 113, 114
Murrow, Edward R., 84, 130, **130**
museums, 81, 95-96, 98, 99, 100, 102, 103, 105, 118
music, 84-86, 88
Nags Head, 93, **119**
name, origin of, 109
Nantahala Gorge, 107
Nantahala National Forest, 106-107, 111
Nantahala River, **13**

national forests, 92, 104, 106-107, 111
natural resources, 74, 117
Natural Science Center, 99
naval stores, 36
Neuse River, 13, 112
New Bern, 32, 33, 39, 96, 121, 124, 125
New River, 104
newspapers, 77, 117, 125
nicknames, 7, 42, 61, 107, 109
Noland, Kenneth, 130
Nordenholz, Fred, 67
North Carolina Botanical
   Gardens, 98-99, 123
North Carolina School of
   Science and Mathematics, 71
North Carolina School of the
   Arts, 71, 126
North Carolina State Art
   Society, 81
North Carolina State University, **71**, 72, 77, 87, 116, 119
North Carolina Symphony
   Orchestra, 84, **85**, 119
North Carolina Zoological Park, 99, 123
Oconaluftee Indian Village, 121
Ocracoke Island, 16, 34, **94**
O. Henry. See Porter, William
   Sydney
Old Salem, 89, **100**, 121

Old Time Fiddler's Convention, 88
Orton Plantation, 97, **138**
outdoor dramas, 86-87, 93, 101, 119
Outer Banks, 12, **12**, 16, 27, 29, 33, 92-93, 94, 111, **119**
Page, Walter Hines, 130
Pamlico Indians, 27
Pamlico River, 13, 14
Pamlico Sound, **49**
Parkway Playhouse, 105
patriots, 38
Pea Island National Wildlife Refuge, 93
Pearson Falls, **6**
Penn, John, 130
Perry, Gaylord, 87, 130
Perry, Jim, 87
Petty, Richard, 88
Pfeiffer College, 116
Phelps Lake, 112
Piedmont, 10, 11, 13, **14**, 17, 20-21, 22, 37, 43, 57, 74, 111, 112, 113, 114
Pilot Mountain State Park, 101
Pinehurst, 88, 123
pirates, 33, **33**
Pisgah National Forest, 104, 111
Pittman, Hobson, 82
Polk, James K., 43, 102, 103, 121, 125, 131, **131**
Polk, Leonidas, 131
Polk, Leonidas L., 58, 131
population, 20-21, 35, 43, 51, 110-111, **136**
Populist party, 58
Porter, William Sydney, **82**, 83, 131
products, principal, 117, **136**
Pungo Lake, 112
Qualla Cherokee Indian Boundary, 21-22, 44, 105
radio stations, 77, 117
railroads, 45, 53, 117, 125
Raleigh, 10, 20, 21, 39, 44, 50, 59, 71, 76, **89**, 98, **98**, 109, 110, 116, 117, 118, 119, 123, 125, 126

Raleigh, Sir Walter, 28-30, 86, 124, 131, **131**
Randolph, E. E., Mrs., 110
Read, Mary, 33, **33**
Reconstruction, 51-53, 126
recreation, **13**, 94, 119, **119**
Reed, Conrad, 101
Reed Gold Mine, 101, 125
regionalism, 22-23
Regulators, 37, 99, 125
Reid, J. R., 87
Reidsville, 76, 99
religion, 23
reptile, state, 109
Research Triangle Park, 64, **66**, 77, 111, 126
Revels, Hiram, 131, **131**
Revolutionary War, 7, 37-38, 42, 97
Reynolds, R. J., Co., 67, 99, 127
Reynolds House, 118
Rhine, Joseph Banks, 131
rivers, 13, 42, 112
roads, **44**, 61, 117, **136**
Roanoke Island, 12, 29-30, **29**, 50, 86, 93, 119, 120, 124
Roanoke Rapids, 95
Roanoke Rapids Reservoir, 112
Roanoke River, 13, 112
Robbinsville, 85
Rockingham, 101
Rocky Mount, 95, 110, 116
Rodanthe, **16**
St. Paul's Church, 95
St. Peter's Church, **5**
St. Thomas Celebration of the Arts, 88
Salem, 35, **35**, 99
Salem Female Academy, **45**
Salisbury, **50**, 100, 116
Saluda, 89
Sanford, Terry, 64, 131
scalawags, 51
Scott, W. Kerr, 64
Scruggs, Earl, 85, 131
sea oats, **4**
segregation, 60, 65, 126
service industries, 76-77

sharecroppers, 58
Shelby, 76, 103
shell, state, 109
Shenandoah National Park, 122
Sherman, William T., 50
Sime, Dave, 87
Singletary Lake State Park, 97
"sit-ins," **64**, 126
Slaughter, Enos, 131
slavery, 36, 47-48
Smith, Betty, **82**, 83-84
Smithfield, 39, 50
Snow Camp, 86
song, state, 110
Sons of Liberty, 37
sounds, 12
South Carolina, 10, 31, 35
Southport, 97, 117
Soybean Festival, 88
Speight, Francis, 82
Spivey's Corner, 89
sports, **86**, 87-88, 119
Sports Hall of Fame, 88
Spruce Pine, 105
Stamp Act, 37
statehood, 38-39, 109
state parks, 92, 104
Statesville, 76
Stevens, J. P., Co., 67, 126
Stone Mountain State Park, 104
Strawberry Festival, 88
Sunday in the Park Festival, 88
Swannanoa, 116
Tannahill, Mary, 81
Tarboro, 39, 95
taxes, 70
Taylor, Lawrence, 87, 119
Teach, Edward, 33
television stations, 77, 117
tenant farming, 58
Tennessee, 10, 11
Thalian Hall, 96
theater, 86-87, 106, 119
Thomasville, 76
Thompson, David, 87
tobacco, 35-36, 56-57, 62, 66, **72**, 73
topography, 113, **133**, **137**

Topsail Island, 94
Tories, 38
Town Creek Indian Mound State
    Historic Site, 101
trade, 66, 73
Trail of Tears, 43-44
transportation, 42, 45, 77, 117,
    136
trees, 14, 74, 114
    state, **108**, 109
Tryon, William, 96
Tryon Palace, 96, **96**, 121
Tsali, Chief, 44
Turner, Nat, 47, 48
Tuscarora Indians, 27, 32-33
Tuscarora War, 33, 125
Tyler, Anne, 84
Ugly Pick-up Truck Contest, 89
Union Grove, 88
United States Mint, **46**, 102
University of North Carolina,
    42, 65, 72, 77, 81, 87, 116, **116**,
    118, 119, 125
Unto These Hills, 86-87, 119
USS *North Carolina*, 96, 121, **122**

Uwharrie National Forest, 101,
    111
Vance, Zebulon B., 48, 50, 52,
    131, **131**
Vanderbilt, Cornelius, 131
Verrazano, Giovanni da, 28, 123
Virginia, 10, 11, 14, 35
voting, **52**, 60
Waccamaw Lake, 112
Waddell, Hugh, 125
Wake County Courthouse, 39
Wake Forest, 116
Walker, David, 83
Watauga River, 112
Watson, Arthel ''Doc,'' 85
Waxhaw, 101
Waxhaw Indians, 27
Weldon, 45, 95
White, John, 30, **124**
    drawings by, **27**, **29**, 80, **81**
Whiteside Mountain, 106
Whitewater Falls, 106
Wiley, Calvin H., 45-46
Wilkes Grand National Stock
    Race, 88

Williams, Mary Lyde, 80
Wilmington, 12, 34, 38, 45, 50,
    63, 72, 87, 88, 94, 96, 97, 110,
    111, 114, 116, 117, 121
Wilmington Railroad Museum,
    96
Wilson, 73, 88, 116
Wilson, Warren College, 116
Wingate, 116
Wingate College, 116
Winston, 35, 99
Winston-Salem, 20, 21, 65, 67,
    71, 76, 99-100, 110, 116, 118,
    119, 121, 126
Wolfe, Thomas, **82**, 122, 131
World Golf Hall of Fame, 88, 123
World War I, 63
World War II, 63-64, **63**
Worth, Jonathan, 48
Worthy, James, 87
Wright, Orville, 61, 92-93, 126
Wright, Wilbur, 61, 92-93, 126
Wright Brothers National
    Memorial, **93**, 122
Wrightsville Beach, 94

Picture Identifications

Front cover: Pioneer Farmstead, Great Smoky Mountains National Park
Back cover: Charlotte
Pages 2-3: Bodie Island Lighthouse
Page 6: Pearson Falls near Saluda
Pages 8-9: The Great Smoky Mountains as seen from Jackson County
Pages 18-19: Montage of North Carolina residents
Pages 24-25: The baptism of Virginia Dare, the first English child born in America
Pages 40-41: An 1830 drawing of the Dismal Swamp Canal astride the North Carolina-
Virginia border
Pages 54-55: A worker in a North Carolina textile mill in the early 1900s
Page 68: The North Carolina State Capitol
Pages 78-79: *Jamming at the Savoy* by North Carolina native Romare Bearden
Pages 90-91: Pastureland along the Blue Ridge Parkway near Deep Gap
Page 108: Montage showing the state flag, the state tree (pine), the state flower (flowering
dogwood), the state bird (cardinal), and the state mammal (gray squirrel)

About the Author

R. Conrad Stein was born and grew up in Chicago. He began writing
professionally shortly after graduating from the University of Illinois. He is
the author of many books, articles, and short stories written for young
readers. Mr. Stein lives in Chicago with his wife and their daughter Janna.

Picture Acknowledgments

Metro Litho
Oak Forest, IL 60452

DATE DUE
